T
NORTHA_____ _ UN &
BANBURY JUNCTION
RAILWAY

by
Stanley C. Jenkins
BA, Cert. Ed, MA

THE OAKWOOD PRESS

© 1990 Oakwood Press and Stanley C. Jenkins

ISBN 0 85361 390 7

Typesetting by Gem Publishing Company, Brightwell, Wallingford, Oxon

Printed by Alphaprint, Witney, Oxon

All rights reserved. No part of this book may be reproduced or transmitted in any form or by any means, electronic or mechanical, including photo-copying, recording or by any information storage and retrieval system, without permission from the Publisher in writing.

A Johnson small-boilered class '2', 0−6−0 No. 3695 stands beside the simple island platform at Blisworth SMJ station; the LNWR main line can be seen to the left. The date of the photograph is probably about 1925.   *Douglas Thompson*

Published by
The OAKWOOD PRESS
P.O.Box 122, Headington, Oxford

Contents

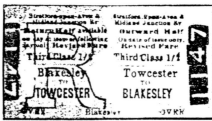

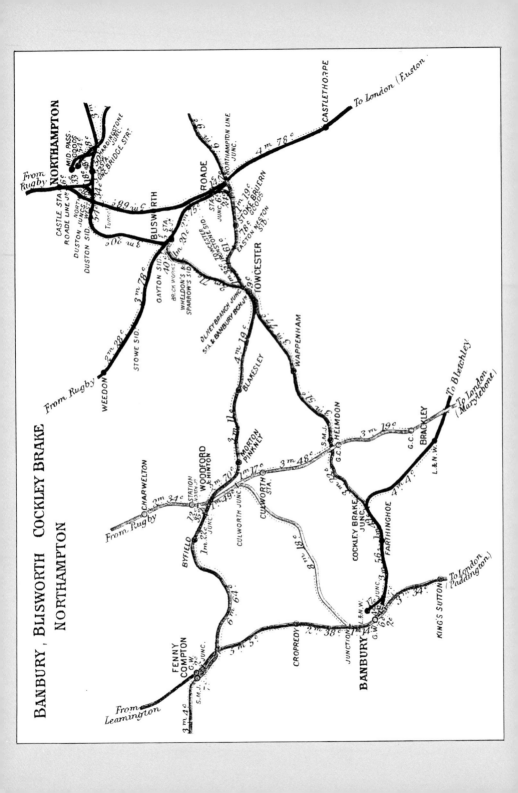

BANBURY, BLISWORTH COCKLEY BRAKE NORTHAMPTON

Introduction

Running from Blisworth in Northamptonshire, to Cockley Brake Junction, near Banbury, the Northampton & Banbury Junction Railway reached neither Northampton, nor Banbury, but its grand-sounding name proclaimed to the World that this was a main line that might have been! Projected during the "Second Railway Mania" of the mid-1860s, the line never rose above secondary status, and in its last years the N&BJR company joined forces with the neighbouring Stratford-upon-Avon & Midland Junction Railway, becoming (in popular memory) an integral part of that interesting minor company. In reality, the N&BJR was quite distinct from the Stratford company, and although several worthy books have been published on the S&MJR, the story of the Northampton & Banbury Junction has not yet been told. It is hoped, in view of this omission, that the present volume will help to fill a gap in the railway history of the Banbury region by focussing attention on one of the smaller English pre-grouping companies. The story encompasses Banbury Merton Street (and a short section of the Buckinghamshire Railway between Banbury and Cockley Brake) but the S&MJR is not covered in great detail; readers wishing to know more about the Towcester to Stratford line should refer to *The Stratford-upon-Avon & Midland Junction Railway* by J.M. Dunn.

Although this work does not pretend to be a work of great scholarship, it is based upon contemporary sources, and for the benefit of local historians who may wish to follow their own studies a limited number of footnotes have been included. These are, however, only intended as a general guide and there has been no attempt to provide a source reference for every fact or figure. Instead, key sources are indicated at the end of certain paragraphs, and it is envisaged that this method of citation will help potential scholars without over-burdening the text with expensive and unnecessary notes. It should be stressed that this is essentially a compromise solution, and the sources cited are only those that lend themselves to easy notation (such as Acts of Parliament); timetables, working notices and certain non-printed sources are not cited.

Stanley C. Jenkins
Witney, Oxfordshire
1989

An exterior view of Blisworth N&BJR station; note the train, which can be seen in one of the station's two terminal platforms. Although opened to public traffic in 1866, it appears that the simple Italianate station building was not finished until 1871.

Lens of Sutton

Ex-MR class '2F', 0–6–0 No. 3696 waits at Blisworth, while the short lived Ro-Railer vehicle has just arrived in the opposite platform; the year is 1932. L.R.G.P. Collection, Courtesy David and Charles

Chapter One

Origins of the Northampton & Banbury Junction (1840–1866)

Situated somewhat uncomfortably in an ill-defined region that is too far north to be part of the Home Counties, too far west to belong to East Anglia and too far south to be truly part of the Midlands, Northamptonshire cannot easily be categorised. It is, in truth, an enigmatic county — a result, perhaps, of its early history as a "border" area between Mercia, Wessex and East Anglia (and later between the English and the Danes). Scenically, these political divisions are echoed by differing types of landscapes; the Soke of Peterborough, for example, is a flat fenland region, while the Oolitic limestone found in the west of the county imparts a West Country air.

Formation of the Buckinghamshire Railway

In railway terms, Northamptonshire is equally diverse, and several of the old companies penetrated its irregularly-shaped borders. First on the scene was the London & Birmingham Railway which, in April 1838, opened lines between London and Denbigh Hall and between Birmingham and Rugby. Further progress was impeded by the great tunnel at Kilsby, but on 17th September, 1838 the 1 mile 666 yard tunnel was completed and the London to Birmingham line was opened throughout.

Having established itself in the Northamptonshire/Buckinghamshire/ Oxfordshire area the London & Birmingham attempted to consolidate its position by backing or promoting various extensions and branch lines, among them a cross-country route from Blisworth to Peterborough. Further south, a company known as the Buckinghamshire Railway was building a line from the L&B main line at Bletchley to Banbury, together with a shorter branch from Claydon Junction to Oxford. Conceived for "political" rather than purely economic reasons, the Buckinghamshire Railway was designed to counteract the rival Oxford & Rugby line, while ensuring that Great Western interests would be unable to penetrate London & Birmingham territory. The scheme had originated in 1847 when two nebulous projects — the Buckingham & Brackley and the Oxford & Bletchley Railways — had combined forces to strengthen their respective undertakings. Meanwhile, in another merger, the mighty London & Birmingham had itself merged with the Grand Junction Railway to form the London & North Western Railway.

As a result of these complex developments, the LNWR emerged as a major force in the region, and this newly-created company was able to provide no less than £450,000 to finance the Buckinghamshire Railway's two-pronged attack on the GWR at Banbury and Oxford.

Solidly supported by the LNWR, the Buckinghamshire Directors started building their railway in April 1847, and construction proceeded apace throughout the next few months. At the half-yearly meeting held at Euston in 1849 the shareholders were informed that "£716,798 6s. 3d. had been spent on the works up to 31st December, 1848", and at the next general meeting the Buckinghamshire Railway Chairman was able to report that the works were "proceeding in a satisfactory manner on the line from Bletchley to Banbury". The line to Oxford was in a "forward state" and work on the stations was under way, although, as an economy measure, these new buildings would be "reduced to the smallest scale consistent with efficient traffic accommodation". It was reported that the completed line would be double from Bletchley to the divergence of the Oxford and Banbury lines at Claydon Junction, and single thereafter, "providing, however, a double line for an adequate distance at each important station". Ending the meeting on an optimistic note, the Chairman claimed that the railway "would improve the country through which it ran to a great extent" and, as "the land was rendered more fruitful ... so would the value of the railway shares increase"![1]

With lines from Bletchley to Banbury and from Blisworth to Peterborough open or in an advanced state of construction, the London & North Western Board was willing to support a company known as the Northampton & Banbury Railway which, on 9th July, 1849, had obtained an Act for construction of a connecting line between the Peterborough and Banbury routes. Leaving the Buckinghamshire Railway at a point known as "Cockley Brake", the proposed line would have run north-eastwards through relatively difficult terrain to a junction with the Peterborough line at Gayton Wharf, near Blisworth. The LNWR agreed to build the railway and lease it when completed; the period for completion of the works was five years.

With support from the LNWR guaranteed, the Northampton & Banbury Junction Railway seemed destined for early success, but unfortunately, external events intervened before this promising scheme could be brought to a successful conclusion.

The middle 1840s were a time of acute social and economic crisis. At the end of 1845 an unforeseen failure of the potato crop had deprived the labouring classes of a major addition to their diet, and when, in 1846, both the potato and corn harvests failed the European economic system was thrown into utter chaos. On top of this, a partial failure of the American cotton crop caused the price of cotton to rise, and all of this happened at a time when most of Britain's surplus capital was tied up in new (and often unnecessary) railway schemes. Indeed, so much capital had been poured into railway construction that a crisis of some kind was bound to follow the railway boom; as it was, the collapse of the railway stock market coincided with a vicious upward spiral in the price of corn, and in these grave and unhappy circumstances the Northampton & Banbury Railway Company was unable to raise its authorised capital.

Opening to Banbury

In the meantime the Buckinghamshire Railway was making good progress with its lines to Banbury and Oxford, although the work of construction did not proceed without incident. In February 1850 The Railway Times reported a mishap that had recently taken place on the unfinished line from Bletchley:

> The Kennedy, which has been used as a ballast engine, is injured, and from being unfit for work, is laid aside. The injury was caused from the want of water in the

boiler, and it is fortunate that it did not lead to worse results. The disaster occurred when the engine was in charge of the stoker and during the absence of the ordinary engine-man.[2]

By March 1850 the works were so far advanced that a party of Directors and officials were able to travel through from Bletchley to Banbury aboard a special train. The new railway was inspected by Captain Wynne, HM Inspector of Railways, on 19th April, but he refused to "pass" the line for opening until various connections at Banbury and elsewhere had been completed. A further inspection was carried out by Captain Laffan on 29th April, and permission for opening having been granted, the Buckingham-shire Railway commenced operations on 1st May, 1850.

The opening of the railway was celebrated in style, and contemporary press accounts reveal that large crowds watched the departure of the "First Train" from Banbury at 6.30 am. The next departures were at 9.45 am and 1.45 pm, and both carried considerable numbers of first day travellers. The last train of the day left Banbury at 5.00 pm; the neighbourhood of the station had, by that time, taken on the appearance of a fair, with flags, stalls and a brass band all much in evidence!

The original train service provided four up and four down trains, all services being worked by the London & North Western Railway as previously agreed. Goods and coal traffic was carried from 15th May, 1850, while from 1st October the branch from Claydon Junction to Islip was opened. The Buckinghamshire Railway did not, as yet, reach its goal of Oxford, but on 2nd December the opening of a further 2½ miles of line between Islip and "Oxford Road" brought the new railway within sight of its destination.

The company had originally intended to reach Oxford by means of running powers over the rival Great Western Railway, but when the latter refused to allow access over its own metals, the Buckinghamshire Railway was obliged to build an independent line, running parallel to the GWR as far as Rewley Road. Here, a small wooden terminus was opened on 20th May, 1851, and the completion of the line was celebrated in the usual way, with glowing speeches and a great banquet. Meanwhile, the LNWR had agreed to take out a 999-year lease, promising the Buckinghamshire company's shareholders a guaranteed dividend of 4½ per cent of all surplus profits. However, the Buckinghamshire Board continued to meet, and its reports to the shareholders provide many interesting glimpses of the railway in operation.

In August 1851, it was revealed that between 5th May and 3rd August over 7072 passengers had been conveyed to London to visit the Great Exhibition many of them from Banbury or Oxford; additionally, the line had carried 31,300 tons of coal to Banbury, Oxford and intermediate stations.[3] Unfortunately, the Buckinghamshire Railway was not as profitable as had been hoped, and subsequent Directors' reports suggest that the proprietors of the line were unhappy with the way in which the LNWR was running the railway. Eventually, after repeated complaints about poor services and rising fares, Mr Ross Mangles — a North Western representative on the Board — was forced to admit that, in guaranteeing a dividend to the Buckinghamshire shareholders, the LNWR was actually out of pocket and had to "work the line as best they could". The local company's Directors soon lost any real interest in their line, and as early as 1856 it was stated that the Board met "only to see that the dividend was paid".[4]

Formation of the Northampton & Banbury Junction Railway

Although the subsequent history of the Buckinghamshire Railway was not as happy as had once been anticipated, the ease with which the promoters had built and opened their line must have been a source of much irritation for the unfortunate Northampton & Banbury supporters — whose own line remained unrealised. There were, nevertheless, tentative proposals for a revival of the abortive 1849 scheme, and these proposals assumed tangible form in the 1860s when — in the middle of a second "Railway Mania" — a group of landowners and entrepreneurs sought Parliamentary consent for a line linking Blisworth and Banbury.

On 6th February, 1863 the promoters petitioned Parliament for leave to bring in "a Bill to authorise the construction of a railway in the county of Northampton, to be called The Northampton & Banbury Junction Railway", and the petition having been presented and read, the Bill itself was read for the first time on 9th February.[5]

The Northampton & Banbury Junction Bill was sent up to the Lords in the following summer, and on 14th July Lord Redesdale reported that the committee appointed to consider the Bill had met and, having examined the Bill, they had found its provisions in order, apart from a minor point of detail concerning "a public road crossing at 12 miles 68 chains in the parish of Stuchbury". His Lordship explained that the Board of Trade had recommended that a steeper approach road of 1 in 13 should be allowed because "the altered road" would be "somewhat better as regard slope" than the existing road.[6]

On 23rd July, 1863 *The Journal of the House of Commons* noted that the lower house had agreed to the Lords amendment, and the clerk was then ordered "to carry the Bill up to the Lords". Finally, on 22nd July, 1863, the Bill authorising "construction of a railway in the county of Northampton to be called The Northampton & Banbury Junction Railway" received the Royal Assent.

Some Details of the Act

The resulting Act (26 & 27 Vic. cap. 220) provided consent for an 18 mile railway from Blisworth to Cockley Brake, at which point the new branch would form a junction with the existing Buckinghamshire Railway. The authorised line was defined as:

A Railway commencing in the parish of Blisworth by a junction with the siding on the west side of the London and North Western Railway, at or near the Blisworth station of that Railway, and terminating in the parish of Gretworth, otherwise Greatworth, by a junction with the Banbury Extension of the Buckinghamshire Railway, about forty yards eastward of the bridge which carries the public road from Marston St Lawrence to Farthinghoe over the said Banbury Extension Railway in the county of Northampton.[7]

AN

A C T

To authorize the Construction of a Railway in the County of Northampton, to be called "The Northampton and Banbury Junction Railway;" and for other purposes.

[Royal Assent, 28th July, 1863.]

WHEREAS the construction of the Railway hereinafter described Preamble. would be of great public and local advantage:

And whereas the several persons in this Act named, with others, are willing at their own expense to construct the same and it is expedient that they be incorporated with the necessary powers for that purpose:

And whereas plans and sections showing the line and levels of the Railway, and the lands by this Act authorized to be acquired for the purposes thereof, and books of reference to such plans, containing

Reproduction of the front page of the Act authorising the Northampton and Banbury Junction Railway.

The Act named Alexander Beattie, Cooke Baines, William Gregory, Robert Stanton Wise and George Eady as the first Directors, and these gentlemen were authorised to raise the sum of £140,000 in fourteen thousand shares of ten pounds each". Additionally, the company was allowed to borrow a further sum of £46,000 when the whole of the share capital was subscribed; the number of Directors would be five, and the qualification for a seat on the Board was fixed at thirty shares. A time limit of five years was set for completion of the works, while the period for compulsory purchase of land would be three years.

The Act went into meticulous detail with respect to the various categories of traffic that might be carried over the Northampton & Banbury Junction Railway, and an elaborate scale of charges was stipulated; "stones for building, pitching and paving . . . brick, tiles, slates, clay, sand, ironstone, pig-iron, bar-iron, rod-iron, hoop-iron and all other similar descriptions of wrought iron and iron castings", for example, would be chaged at the rate not exceeding one penny, but "if conveyed in carriages belonging to the company" an additional sum "not exceeding one half-penny" would be charged. If these carriages were "propelled by an engine belonging to the company" a further sum, not exceeding three farthings, would be charged, subject, however, to a maximum charge "not exceeding two pence per ton per mile". Similarly, "all sugar, grain, corn, flour, hides, dye-woods, earthenware, timber, deals, metals (except iron), nails, anvils, vices, and chains" would be charged at a rate not exceeding two pence per ton per mile, but if conveyed in the company's own vehicles an additional sum not exceeding three farthings would be levied, and if propelled by an engine belonging to the company a further three farthings would be charged, subject to an upper limit of three pence per ton per mile inclusive of all tolls and charges.[8]

As far as passenger traffic was concerned, the Act stated that the maximum rate of charge to be made by the company, "including the tolls for the use of the railway, and of carriages, and for locomotive power" would be no more than 3d. per mile for first class travellers, 2d. for second class passengers, and 1½d. for third class bookings. Interestingly, the latter figure was above the "Parliamentary" rate of one penny per mile, which meant that the railway, when opened, would be compelled to run one train in each direction as a sort of "Fourth class special" conveying holders of cheap 1d. a mile Parliamentary tickets.

133—EAST AND WEST JUNCTION.

Incorporated by 27 and 28 Vic., cap. 76 (23rd June, 1864), to construct a line from Towcester, on the Northampton and Banbury, to Old Stratford, on the Honeybourne branch of the Great Western. Length, 40½ miles. Capital, 300,000l., in 20l. shares, and 100,000l. on loan. Meetings in April and October.

*No. of Directors—*9; minimum, 3; quorum, 3. *Qualification,* 500l.

DIRECTORS;

Chairman—SIR CUSACK P. RONEY, Bart., 15, Langham Place, London, W.

Sir Charles Mordaunt, Bart, M.P., Palace | Mathew Malcolm, Esq.
Hotel, Buckingham Gate, S.W. | William John Addison, Esq.

Extract from Bradshaw's Shareholders' Manual for 1864.

These provisions were little more than legal formalities, and it should be stressed that identical or near-identical provisions were inserted into many other railway Acts passed during the 19th century. Nevertheless, the proposed carriage tolls provide an interesting glimpse of the types of traffic that were expected to flow over the railway, and for this reason some of the provisions have been summarised in *Table 1* (below).

Table 1

PROPOSED SCALE OF CHARGES PER MILE ON THE N&BJR, 1863

Type of Traffic	basic rate of charge	toll for use of vehicle	toll for use of engine	maximum rate of charge
Stones, bricks, tiles, slates, clay, sand, iron-stone, iron-ore, pig-iron, bar-iron and wrought iron, etc. (per ton)	1d.	½d.	¾d.	2d.
Sugar, grain, corn, flour, hides, dye-woods, earthenware, timber, deals, metals (except iron, nails, anvils, vices and chains) (per ton)	2d.	¾d.	¾d.	3d.
Cotton, wool, drugs, manufactured goods, fish, etc. (per ton)	3d.	1d.	¾d.	4d.
Carriages and other road vehicles	4d.	1d.	1d.	5d.
Horses, mules & other beasts of draught	3d.	1d.	1d.	4d.
Cows, bulls and other cattle	2d.	½d.	¾d.	2½d.
Calves, pigs, sheep and other small animals	½d.	¼d.	¼d.	1d.
Boilers, cylinders or machinery between 4 and 8 tons	—	—	—	6d.
First class passengers	—	—	—	3d.
Second class passengers	—	—	—	2d.
Third class passengers	—	—	—	1½d.

Other parts of the Northampton & Banbury Junction Act dealt with the proposed junctions with the LNWR at Blisworth and Cockley Brake, and (as usual in such circumstances) the larger company's rights were carefully safeguarded. The Act stipulated that the junctions would only be made:

At such places as the London and North Western Railway Company (being also lessees of the Buckinghamshire Railway and its Banbury Extension) shall agree to, and not otherwise, unless the London and North Western Railway Company shall, by writing, under their common seal, agree to some other mode of communication; and all works required for effecting such junctions upon or affecting the lands or works of the London and North Western Railway Company, and the Buckinghamshire Railway Company, shall be made according to the plans first approved by the engineer for the time being of the London and North Western Railway Company, and shall be executed under his superintendence and control, and at the expense of the Company.[9]

Further provision dealt with the erection of signals at the proposed junctions, and again, the LNWR was given wide-ranging powers; the Act provided that the North Western could:

> Erect, maintain, and alter such signals and conveniences incident to the junctions, and appoint and remove such watchmen, switchmen, or other persons as they may deem necessary for the prevention of danger to, detention of, or interference with the traffic at or near the said junctions.

Moreover, the Act stated that the working and management of such signals, and the control and direction of all watchmen, pointsmen, or other persons, would belong *exclusively* to the London & North Western Railway — even if the men concerned were working on Northampton & Banbury Junction property. Furthermore, money for "erecting, altering, repairing, and maintaining" the junction signals, together with the wages of all "watchmen, pointsmen and other persons" would be paid by the Northampton & Banbury Junction Railway "at the end of every half-year".

The First Half-Yearly Meeting

The first half-yearly meeting of the newly-constituted company was held in the N&BJ offices at 6 Victoria Street, Westminster, in April 1864, with Mr Cooke Baines in the chair. Mr Theobald, the company Secretary, read an optimistic report which congratulated the shareholders on the success off their recent application to Parliament. The report stated that "a direct line of railway between the large and important towns of Northampton and Banbury" had now been authorised, and when completed, this new railway was expected to become "a main line of communication" connecting the east of England with Wales.

It was anticipated that iron ore would form a significant proportion of the new line's traffic, and, when the Northamptonshire ironstone quarries were placed in contact with South Wales, it was hoped that "upwards of 400,000 tons of . . . Northamptonshire iron ore" would be carried over the N&BJR each year. The report added that a contract for construction of the railway had been concluded, "thereby ensuring the immediate commencement of the works".[10]

A further item of business dealt with at this first meeting concerned the re-election of officers and Directors. It was agreed that a new five man board, consisting of Alexander Beattie, Cooke Baines, George Eady, Jaspar W. John and C.J. Tahourdin would be formed, and at the same time W.H. Wilson and A.T. Bowser were elected as auditors.

As far as can be ascertained, the new Directors were not local people, and this underlines a significant point that might be made in connection with the Northampton & Banbury Junction Railway — the company was a specu-lative venture, and its promoters hoped to grow rich by carrying long distance iron ore traffic. There was little interest in purely local traffic, and although the new railway would obviously help the economy of Towcester and other places *en route* to Banbury, this aim was of secondary importance in relation to the overall scheme.

Alexander Beattie — the N&BJR Chairman — was a doctor of medicine with a penchant for railway investments, and *Bradshaw's Shareholders Manual & Guide* reveals that he was involved with several other railway companies, including the Carnarvon & Llanberis and the South Eastern Railway. His address was given as 45 Porchester Terrace, Hyde Park, London, but he also resided at 'Summerhill', Chislehurst, Kent. George Eady was similarly involved with other railways besides the Northampton & Banbury Junction, and it is interesting to find that he was solicitor of the Carnarvon & Llanberis Railway in North Wales.[11]

It appears, from this evidence, that Messrs Beattie, Eady, Baines and their co-Directors may have seen the Northampton & Banbury Junction Railway merely as one of a diverse number of investments. Such men were clearly willing to risk their own money when the economic climate was favourable, but in times of financial stringency speculative investors often lacked the personal commitment needed to see projects through to a successful conclusion, and for these reasons the N&BJR scheme risked finding itself in serious trouble. For the moment, however, the scheme seemed destined for early success, and having obtained their Act, the promoters were eager to begin construction of their railway.

It was reported, in February 1865, that the "works between Blisworth and Towcester were being vigorously proceeded with", and there was "every probability that the line between those two places would be completed by the end of . . . the year". Indeed, the N&BJR Directors were so confident that they expected the entire line to be ready for opening "by the Spring of 1866". A few weeks later, on 8th April, 1865, *The Railway Times* announced that the Northampton & Banbury Junction Railway had made arrangements with the London & North Western which, "by increasing the running powers of the company would materially increase traffic on the line".

Meanwhile, the N&BJR promoters, not content with running a useful, but minor cross-country branch, were initiating a series of more grandiose projects which, if successfully completed, would transform the original Blisworth to Banbury line into an integral part of a major trunk route between the Northamptonshire iron producing area and South Wales. Such a line, when completed, would enable good quality iron ore to reach the Welsh coalfields where it could profitably be smelted prior to export overseas.

In February 1865 the Northampton & Banbury Junction Railway had applied to Parliament for Powers to deviate a small portion of the 1863 line "and extend it to the town of Banbury", and the new Bill was read for the first time on 21st February, 1865 and ordered to be read a second time. In connection with this scheme, the company also sought Powers to construct extensions to Chipping Norton and Blockley, and the Northampton & Banbury Junction (Extension) Bill received its first reading on 22nd February, 1865. Both of the 1865 Bills were ultimately successful, and as a result of their latest application to Parliament the N&BJR promoters obtained wide-ranging additional powers.

The Acts of 1865

The Northampton & Banbury Railway (Branch) Act (28 & 29 Vic. cap. 361) authorised the construction of a branch connecting the original N&BJR line to the Northampton & Peterborough line of the London & North Western Railway. To pay for this and other works, the company was empowered to raise additional share capital of £145,000 "by preference shares or otherwise", while borrowing on mortgage a further sum of £45,300. Three years were allowed for the compulsory purchase of land, and the time limit set for completion of the works was five years.[12] An agreement between the N&BJR and North Western companies was scheduled to the Act, and this agreement clarified the position regarding running powers over the LNWR between Cockley Brake Junction and Banbury; a further provision provided for N&BJ trains to use the North Western and Great Western stations at Banbury.

The Northampton & Banbury Railway (Extension) Act (28 & 29 Vic. cap. 362) provided for the construction of lines from Banbury to Blockley, with a branch to Chipping Norton, and for convenience, these new lines were treated as four railways. "Railway No. 1" was the Chipping Norton branch, while "Railway No. 2", "Railway No. 3" and "Railway No. 4" together constituted the main line to Blockley. To finance this ambitious scheme the company was empowered to raise a further £500,000 by preference or other shares, and to borrow an additional £166,000; the time for completion was again five years.[13]

The Northampton & Banbury Junction supporters were now playing for high stakes, and if their schemes were completed as planned, the company would be a force to be reckoned with in the railway world. A project of such magnitude attracted considerable attention from publications such as *The Railway Times*, and on 12th August, 1865 this influential investors' journal printed a very full report of a N&BJR meeting that had been held at the company's London office on the previous Saturday. The meeting was chaired by Dr Beattie, and the first item of business was the Directors' report:

> The report stated that the works were progressing satisfactorily, and there was reason to believe that the railway would be opened for traffic by the time originally comtemplated. An Act was obtained in the last session for making an extension line from Chipping Norton to Banbury, and running powers were secured over the Buckinghamshire line and part of the London & North Western, by which they would be enabled to convey iron ore from Northamptonshire to South Wales. Running powers were confirmed by Parliament, and also the making of a half mile branch to the Northampton & Peterborough at Northampton. The whole length of the line would be 51½ miles. They would ask the proprietors for power to raise capital on five per cent preference shares authorised by the company's Branch Act, 1865, and also by their Extension Act, 1865. The report of Mr Collister, the engineer, stated that the entire line would be completed by the Autumn of 1866.[14]

In moving the adoption of the report, Dr Beattie warmly congratulated the Directors on "the success of their exertions in obtaining the extension . . . from Banbury to Blockley, which would have the effect of conferring great local benefit upon the district through which it would pass, and ultimately be of great advantage to the through traffic in coal and cattle from South Wales to Northampton and Banbury, while it would afford the means of transporting a great deal of iron ore to South Wales." The other extension, from Banbury to Chipping Norton, would, suggested Dr Beattie, be of similar importance in that it would give "the shortest possible route to South Wales,

Cheltenham and Gloucester". The Chairman then referred to the Severn Junction Railway which — when completed — would provide a useful link with Monmouthshire. The report of the Engineer was, he thought, "satisfactory", and it was hoped that the line would be completed "within the period originally anticipated". Having passed these observations, Dr Beattie added that some of his colleagues resided on the spot, and were more conversant with the "advantages that would accrue, both locally and generally, from the construction of the proposed works".

The next speaker was Mr H.J. Sheldon, of Brailes House, Shipton-on-Stour, who had recently been elected to the N&BJR Board of Directors. Living, as he did, between Banbury and Blockley, he was "well acquainted with the wants of the locality", and could therefore "bear evidence to the great requirement there had been", ever since he could remember, "for additional means of communication throughout the district":

> It was a thickly populated agricultural country and a large grazing district, from which many thousand head of cattle might be conveyed to the metropolis if proper communication were afforded. The line would also be a great benefit to the inhabitants of the district, by giving them coal at much less cost . . . he was sure the projected line would secure not only a great local but also a great through traffic.[15]

William Banks — another new Director — agreed with Mr Sheldon that there was a pressing need for improved communications in the districts that would be served by the projected lines. He had himself resided all his life in the neighbourhood of Hereford, and no one could "speak more feelingly than he of the want of communication between Hereford and Northampton". He knew that "enormous quantities of coal were sent by the most circuitous routes to the Northamptonshire district", but when the new lines were open to traffic there would be a much shorter route for both coal and iron ore resulting in "a vast saving of expense".

The meeting ended in an atmosphere of unbounded optimism, and having concluded their ordinary business, the proprietors held a special meeting to discuss the creation of new 5 per cent debenture shares as authorised by the 1865 Acts.

A Further Application to Parliament

Although their original line between Blisworth and Banbury was not yet open, the N&BJR Directors had no intention of finishing their line at Blockley; indeed, the Blockley extension was merely a starting point for *further* lines, and in 1866 the company deposited another Bill, with the intention of completing a link between Blockley and Ross-on-Wye. At Ross, the extension would form a junction with the Ross & Monmouth Railway — a small company authorised, under an Act of 5th July, 1865, to build a 12½ mile line from Monmouth May Hill to Ross-on-Wye.

In retrospect, the early months of 1866 marked the high point of Northampton & Banbury Junction fortunes, and there seemed no reason to suppose that the scheme might founder. With the first section of line almost ready for opening, the latest extension Bill on its way through Parliament, and the prospect of ultimate support from the Midland or Great Western companies, Dr Beattie and his Board now viewed themselves as major players in the great game of railway politics.

The half-yearly meeting held at Victoria Street on 28th February, 1866 was another optimistic gathering; the Directors report stated that "great progress was being made with the works", and the portion of line between Blisworth and Towcester was expected to be open by the following April. The remaining section of the original line was less advanced, but it was confidently expected that "the whole of the line would be completed by the end of the year".[16]

The next item on the agenda was the re-election of Directors, and with this formality safely out of the way, the proprietors elected an important new-comer to the Board in the person of the Right Honourable Lord Ernest Bruce MP. Significantly, Lord Ernest was, like Dr Beattie, intimately connected with various other railways, among them the Berks & Hants — a line linked closely to the Great Western.

Opening to Towcester

With Northampton & Banbury Junction ambitions now centred firmly on South Wales, there was little incentive for the company to lavish attention on the five miles long Blisworth to Towcester line — which was, after all, nothing more than a branch in its existing form. The railway was neverthe-less complete, and on Saturday 28th April, 1866 *The Railway Times* printed the following brief note:

NORTHAMPTON & BANBURY JUNCTION — The portion of this line between Blisworth, on the London & North Western, and Towcester, having been inspected and passed by Colonel Rich, will be opened for traffic in a few days.[17]

It seems that public opening took place on the following Monday, but what should have been a happy event was overshadowed when, less than two months later, on 10th May, 1866, the great banking firm of Overend & Gurney ceased trading. The results were catastrophic, and with the bank rate standing at 10 per cent the Victorian financial system was thrown into disorder. New companies such as the Northampton & Banbury Junction were unable to raise their authorised capital, and in these unhappy circum-stances it seemed that the N&BJR company would have to abandon its expensive extension schemes. More seriously, one of the victims of the crash was Mr Shrimpton, who had secured the main contract for construction of the Towcester to Cockley Brake line.[18] It was reported that Mr Shrimpton's liabilities totalled £220,656, and although the failed contractor's "moderate personal expenses" were referred to with some approval, it was clear to all that the Blisworth to Banbury line was unlikely to be opened in 1866 — or indeed at any time in the immediate future.

Sources for Chapter One

1.   Buckinghamshire Railway Half-Year reports.
2.   *The Railway Times*, February 1850.
3.   *The Railway Times*.
4.   *The Railway Times*.

5. *The Journal of the House of Commons*, 9th February, 1863.
6. *The Journal of the House of Lords*, 14th July, 1863.
7. Northampton & Banbury Junction Act (26 & 27 Vic. cap. 220).
8. *Ibid.*
9. *Ibid.*
10. Northampton & Banbury Junction Half-Year Report, April 1864.
11. *Bradshaw's Shareholders Manual*, 1864.
12. Northampton & Banbury Railway (Branch) Act 1865 (28 & 29 Vic. cap. 361).
13. Northampton & Banbury Railway (Extension) Act 1865 (28 & 29 Vic. cap. 362).
14. *The Railway Times*, 12th August, 1865, p. 1027.
15. *Ibid.* p. 1027.
16. Northampton & Banbury Junction Half-Year Report, February 1866.
17. *The Railway Times*, 28th April, 1866, p. 509.
18. *The Railway Times*, 10th July, 1869, p. 673.

279.—MIDLAND COUNTIES AND SOUTH WALES.

Incorporated by 26 and 27 Vic., cap. 220 (28th July, 1863), to construct a line from Blisworth to Farthinghoe. Capital, 140,000*l.* in 10*l.* shares ; loans, 46,000*l.* compulsory purchase, three years. Completion of works, five years. Works in progress.

By 28 and 29 Vic., cap. 361, Northampton and Banbury Railway (Branch) Act, 1865, the company were empowered to make a branch line to connect their railway with the Northampton and Peterborough line of the London and North Western, and to raise additional capital to the extent of 193,300*l.* ; viz., by shares, 145,000*l.* ; on loan, 48,300*l.* Compulsory powers under this act, three years. Completion of works, five years. Power to enter into traffic arrangements with Great Western. An agreement is scheduled to this act by which the company obtains running powers over the Buckinghamshire line of the London and North Western from Cockley Brake to Banbury, with use of the London and North Western and Great Western stations.

By 28 and 29 Vic., cap. 362, Northampton and Banbury Railway (Extensions) Act, 1865, the company were empowered to extend their railway to Chipping Norton and Blockley, and to raise additional capital to the extent of 666,600*l.*, viz., by shares 500,000*l.* ; on loan, 166,600*l.* Compulsory powers under this act, three years. Completion of works, five years. Works in progress.

By 29 and 30 Vic., cap. 310, Northampton and Banbury Junction Railway Act, 1866, the company were empowered to extend their railway from Blockley to Ross, and to raise additional capital to the extent of 733,000*l.* ; viz., by shares, 550,000*l.* ; on loan, 183,000*l.* Compulsory powers under this act, three years. Completion of works, five years. By this act the company obtain running powers over the Midland Company's lines between Bickford to Tewkesbury, over the Ross and Monmouth, and over the Worcester Dean Forest and Monmouth, between Newport and Monmouth, and the name of the company has been changed from the Northampton and Banbury Junction, to the Midland Counties and South Wales. Total length of line now authorised, 96¼ miles. In April, 1866, that portion of the Railway from Blisworth to Towcester was opened for traffic.

Meetings in February and August.

No. of Directors.—Maximum, 8 ; minimum, 5 ; quorum, when more than five directors, 5 ; when five directors, 3. *Qualification*, 300*l.*

DIRECTORS :

Chairman—The Right Hon. Lord ERNEST BRUCE, M.P., 6, St. George's Place, S.W.

Deputy-Chairman—ALEXANDER BEATTIE, Esq., M.D., 45, Porchester Terrace, Hyde Park, W.

Jasper Wilson Johns, Esq., J.P., Wolverton Park, near Newbury, Hants.
Wm. Laurence Banks, Esq., Watton House, Brecon.
H. J. Sheldon, Esq., Brailes House, Shipston-on-Stour, Worcestershire.

Charles Kelson, Esq., Gresham House, Old Broad Street. E.C.
L. M. Rate, Esq., King's Arms Yard, E.C.
W. R. Drake, Esq., Parliament Street, Westminster, S.W.

OFFICERS.— Sec., J. Wilson Theobald, 6, Victoria Street, Westminster, S.W.; Engs. John Collister, C.E., 28, Great George Street, Westminster, S.W., and Charles Liddell, C.E., 24, Abingdon Street, Westminster, S.W. ; Solicitors, Gregory, Champion and Eady, 18, Park Street, Westminster, S.W., and 12, Clements Inn, W.C.; Bankers, The Union Bank of London (Temple Bar Branch), Chancery Lane, W.C., and The Northamptonshire Banking Company, Northampton.

Offices—6, Victoria Street, Westminster, S.W.

Extract from Bradshaw's Shareholders' Manual of 1867.

56.—BUCKINGHAMSHIRE.

An amalgamation of the BUCKINGHAM AND BRACKLEY, incorporated by 10 Vic., cap. 233 (1846), and of the OXFORD AND BLETCHLEY, incorporated 10 Vic., cap. 82 (1846), under the present title, by 10 and 11 Vic., cap. 236 (1847), with further powers for an extension of the former scheme north to Banbury, and south to Aylesbury—10 miles; Bletchley to Oxford, 31½ miles, with a line from Claydon to a junction with the Great Western, Oxford and Rugby, at Banbury—21¼ miles. Total, 53 miles. Of this there is 21 miles 34 chains single line, and 31 miles 5 chains with double rails. The amount authorised by the extension act of 1847 (450,000*l.*) was provided by the London and North Western. An act was obtained in 1853 to authorise a junction with the Oxford, Worcester, and Wolverhampton, near Oxford. The whole undertaking is leased from 1st July, 1851, for 999 years, under act 11 and 12 Vic., cap. 236, to the London and North Western, at 4 per cent. per annum, with half surplus profits; as, however, the whole of the extension capital is found by the lessees, their actual liability is limited to payment of dividend on the *original* 17½*l.* shares—195,000*l.*

The meeting are held in London, in February and August, for declaration of dividend due 30th June and 31st December.

Scale of Voting.—C. C. C. Act, sec. 75.

Certificates must accompany transfer stock. Registration fee, 2*s.* 6*d.* each deed. The company will transfer 10*s.* of stock.

Director's Qualification, 50 shares—875*l.* stock.

DIRECTORS:

Chairman—Sir HARRY VERNEY, Bart., M.P., South Street, Park Lane, W., and Claydon House, Buckinghamshire.

Robert Benson, Esq., Craven Hill Gardens, Hyde Park, W.

His Grace the Duke of Buckingham, Stowe, Buckinghamshire.

The Right Hon. the Earl of Camperdown, Hill Street, Berkeley Square, W.

Timothy Rhodes Cobb, Esq., Banbury.

Richard Ryder Dean, Esq., Gloucester Place, Portman Square, W.

The Hon. Arthur Kinnaird, M.P., Pall Mall East, S.W.

Matthew Lyon, Esq., Clarendon Square. Leamington.

Thomas Young, Esq., Eaton Square, S.W.

The Directors retire from office in rotation, in the alphabetical order of their names. All eligible for re-election.

OFFICERS.—Sec., William Long; Auditors, Henry Crosfield, Liverpool, and Richard Carter, Buckingham.

Offices—Euston Station, London, N.W.

Extract from the 1866 Bradshaw's Shareholders' Manual.

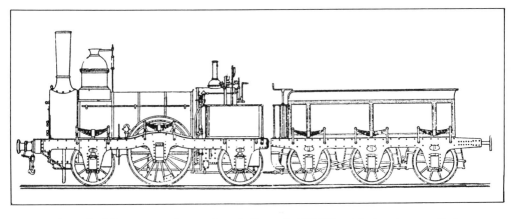

A standard Sharp 2–2–2 locomotive; similar to the N&BJR's original engine, supplied by I.W. Boulton in 1866.

Chapter Two

Opening and Early Years (1866–1872)

The Northampton & Banbury Junction Railway Act of 1866 (29 & 30 Vic. cap. 310) authorised the company to extend its line from Blockley to Ross-on-Wye, and to finance this 34 mile extension the N&BJR was empowered to raise a further share capital of £550,000, and to borrow on mortgage an additional sum of £183,000. The 1866 Act also granted running powers over a section of the Midland Railway between Bickford and Tewkesbury, over the Ross & Monmouth Railway, and over the Worcester, Dean Forest & Monmouth Railway between Newport and Monmouth.[19]

The total length of line authorised by the Acts of 1863, 1865 and 1866 was 96½ miles, and the company's combined share and loan capital now stood at almost £2 million. Under these circumstances, and in view of the projected extensions of the Northampton & Banbury Junction system, it was deemed fitting that a more expansive name should be given to the undertaking, and the company therefore assumed the title "Midland & South Wales Junction Railway".

Motive Power Problems

Unfortunately, the 1866 economic crisis had extinguished all hopes of an immediate commencement of the extension schemes, and with only four miles of their line in operation, the disappointed Midland & South Wales Directors were obliged to focus greater attention on the short section of railway between Blisworth and Towcester. Having appointed Henry Crabtree as traffic superintendent, the company turned its attention to the practicalities of operation. Initial thoughts of an arrangement with the LNWR having been abandoned, the Directors decided to purchase their own locomotives, and a contract was accordingly placed with Neilson & Co. of Glasgow for two 0–4–2Ts and two 0–4–2 tender engines.

In the meantime, there was an urgent need for motive power for use on the Towcester line, and as an interim measure the Directors hired at least one locomotive from I.W. Boulton (a sort of "used engine dealer" who specialised in the buying and selling of second-hand engines). The locomotive involved in this deal was a typical Sharp Roberts 2–2–2 that Mr Boulton had purchased from the LNWR, complete with tender, for £240 in March 1866. Sadly, the engine was not in the best of health, and on arrival at Blisworth it was found to have a cracked cylinder. The 2–2–2 was therefore taken back to Boulton's base at Ashton-under-Lyne, and it appears that a replacement was provided by Boulton's friend Thomas Wheatley (1821–83), who had recently purchased a selection of locomotives from the Monkland & Kirkintilloch Railway near Glasgow. It is conceivable that one, or perhaps two, of these Scottish veterans found their way to Northamptonshire, but precise details remain elusive. It is known, however, that one of the first engines used on the line between Blisworth and Towcester was a decrepit antique known as *The Owl*, and this locomotive may have been a Wheatley-supplied engine.

As we have seen, the opening of the line coincided with the collapse of Messrs Overend & Gurney and a resulting economic crisis, and this meant, in turn, that the company could not afford to pay for its newly-completed Neilson engines*. Faced with these problems vis-à-vis motive power the N&BJR Directors were forced to go cap in hand to the London & North Western, and on 1st October, 1866 a new agreement came into force, whereby the line to Towcester was worked by LNWR locomotives and rolling stock.

Boardroom Changes

The traumas and disappointments of the middle 1860s were accompanied by several boardroom changes as, one by one, the less-committed Directors withdrew their support. New men were brought in to replace the retiring Directors, and, as a result, the composition of the Board changed noticeably between 1864 and the end of the decade. These upheavals are reflected in the following table which shows, at a glance, some of the more important boardroom changes over the sample period 1864–1871.

Table 2

CHANGES IN COMPOSITION OF THE N&BJR BOARD 1864–1871

1864	1867	1870
Alexander Beattie MD	Lord Ernest Bruce MP	Lord Ernest Bruce MP
Cooke Baines	Alexander Beattie MD	Alexander Beattie MD
Robert Stanton Wise	Jasper Wilson Johns	Lachlan M. Rate
William Gregory	William L. Banks	Henry James Sheldon
George James Eady	Henry James Sheldon	Robert Amadeus Heath
	Charles Kelson	Walter Amos Michael
	Lachlan M. Rate	
	W.R. Drake	

NB: The number of Directors was originally fixed at five, but later rose to eight, before the Act of 1870 stipulated a figure of six.

Geographically, the Directors tended to be based in London, and *Bradshaw's Shareholders Manual* suggests that Messrs Beattie, Bruce, Kelson, Rate, Drake, Heath, and Michael all resided in the capital. There was at the same time, a small but significant group of non-London residents, including Jasper Johns of Newbury, William Banks of Brecon, and Henry Sheldon of Brailles (although of these, Jasper Johns also maintained a London residence at 46 Cumberland Street, Hyde Park).

As suggested earlier, many of the Northampton & Banbury Junction promoters appear to have been speculative investors with little obvious interest in the areas through which the railway would run. The non-London Directors, in contrast, appear to have been motivated in a slightly different way, and although they clearly hoped for a good return on their investments, one also detects an underlying sense of public duty in their actions. Henry Sheldon, in particular, had spoken persuasively of the need for improved transport links in the Shipston-on-Stour area at the N&BJR half-yearly meeting in August 1865, and indeed, he had been campaigning for a new

---

* Which were, instead, purchased by the Solway Jn Rly (see *The Solway Junction Railway* published by The Oakwood Press, 1990).

railway before the N&BJR had even been formed. On 10th May, 1862, for example, *The Worcester Herald* had reported a public meeting that had recently been held to discuss a westwards continuation of the railway from Banbury:

> A meeting was held in the George Hotel on Saturday week, H.J. Sheldon Esq., of Brailes in the chair, which was numerously attended by large and influential landowners in the district, to take into consideration the advisability of promoting a line of railway from Banbury by Tadmarton, Traitersford, Mitford Bridge, skirting Shipston and Ilmington, to Honeybourne or Evesham. Such a line would prove of incalculable service to the district through which it passed, and would form a direct communication with Banbury to South Wales. The proposed line has been surveyed, and there is an entire absence of any engineering difficulties of importance, the landowners through whose property it would pass are favourably disposed, it is hoped the matter will be earnestly proceeded with and rewarded by success.[20]

The presence of Henry Sheldon on the N&BJR Board does much to explain the persistent way in which the company pursued its goal of extension to Blockley and beyond, even when that goal seemed a hopelessly distant attainment. In truth, the later 1860s were a particularly black period as far as the Midland Counties & South Wales Junction Railway was concerned because, not only were finances difficult, the initial aim of transporting ore to South Wales had been negated, to a very great extent, by competition from suppliers of cheap Spanish ore which made Northamptonshire iron ore less attractive to the Welsh iron masters.

Undeterred by these vastly changed economic circumstances Dr Beattie, Henry Sheldon, and other members of the Board, stubbornly refused to abandon their scheme, and in 1868 they applied to Parliament for an extension of time for completion of the works. It was admitted that the company had not paid interest on any part of its huge mortgage debts, but as a way out of these problems, it was suggested that the long-suffering debenture holders might be given "a voice in the management of the affairs of the company" and allowed to vote at all meetings. Although this scheme (which would, in effect have enabled stock holders to become the equivalent of share holders) may have gone some way towards solving the company's problems, the 1868 Bill was not proceeded with, and, in a sudden change of plan, the promoters decided to approach the Board of Trade in the hope that an extension of time could be granted without recourse to Parliament.

A Struggling Concern

Meanwhile, the affairs of "The Midland Counties & South Wales Junction Railway" were degenerating into pure farce and, in a state of total bankruptcy, the unfortunate promoters were forced to sell various portions of the Towcester line in an attempt to pay off some of their debts. Indeed, the company was in such distressed condition, that on 5th July, 1869 the following notice was placed in *The Times* newspaper:

> Mr William Anthony Bouler will sell by auction (with the approbation of the Right Hon. the Master of the Rolls, the Judge in whose court this cause is attached,

pursuant to the order therein dated the 18th March, 1869) at the Auction Mart, Tokenhouse Yard, London, tomorrow, the 6th day of July, at two o'clock precisely, in one lot, three plots or parcels of land . . . containing together 10 acres, 0 rods and 32 perches, or thereabouts, and being respectively about 16 chains in length, 36 chains and 4 chains in length, the same being part of the railway between Blisworth and Towcester.[21]

The so-called Midland Counties & South Wales Railway had, by this time, become a laughing stock, and in July 1869 *The Railway Times* commented unfavourably on what it called a "large but most unimportant and unnecessary undertaking". In a lengthy article, published on 24th July, 1869, the journal reminded its readers that the scheme had originated under Parliamentary auspices in 1863, when the N&BJR was incorporated for the stated purpose of construction of an 18 mile line from Blisworth to Farthinghoe. "Of these 18 miles", continued the paper, "only four had been constructed and opened for traffic, but part of those same four miles had recently been sold by order of the Court of Chancery". Warming to its theme, *The Railway Times* then launched into an unusually-strong attack on the entire Northampton & Banbury Junction scheme:

By Act of 1865, without one question being asked by the Legislature as to the actual rate of progress making in the eighteen miles obtained in 1863, the company was authorised to make a deviation to Blisworth so as to connect the original line with the London & North Western system. For this purpose power was obtained to create and issue an additional capital of £145,000 in shares, and £45,300 by debentures. The whole of the share capital authorised by this Act is represented as having been paid up, while the borrowing powers . . . have been fully exercised.

Share and loan capital required for construction of these 18 miles, has thus been paid up to the extent of £449,860; but instead of these 18 miles being constructed and open for traffic, only four have been completed. It would thus appear that the cost of these four miles — seeing that the company acknowledges to have expended, and to be owing, the entire sum of £449,860 — extends to an average of £112,915 per mile. How is this to be accounted for?

The Bill intended to have been submitted in 1868, but withdrawn from Parliamentary cognisance, admitted that the company had not been able to pay interest on any part of its mortgage debt, amounting to £94,900 . . . Notwithstanding that so little had been accomplished under the Act of 1863, and notwithstanding also the application for additional capital in 1865, under pretence of constructing the line to Blisworth, the company succeeded in inducing Parliament to confer upon them what may now be regarded as the most extravagant powers.

For instance, by Act of 1865, extensions to Chipping Norton and to Blockley were authorised, 33 miles in length, at an estimated outlay of £500,000 in shares and £166,000 on mortgage.

By Act of 1866 this same company, with its four miles not then in work, acquired the privilege of making an extension from Blockley to Ross, 34 miles in length, with £550,000 in shares and £183,000 on debentures . . . by these various additions the undertaking has stretched out from 18 miles in length to 96, while its nominal capital is £1,383,300 in shares and £540,600 on mortgage — making in all, with four miles under traffic, a total of £1,923,900.

Couched in such stark terms, the story of the former Northampton & Banbury Junction Railway made sorry reading, but having made the line's promoters look like utter fools (or possibly confidence tricksters) *The Rail-*

way Times proceeded to administer a final series of blows. Recalling that the promoters had approached the Board of Trade for an extension of time, the investors' newspaper passed final judgement on the scheme:

> As this company is not only insolvent, but as, in round numbers, one of its four miles of railway which is open for traffic has been sold by public auction, and is now in possession of a private individual, this is surely not a case in which the Board of Trade should have been called on for an extension of time. Such an application is a waste of time, money, and labour. It is a waste of the public time of the officers of the Board of Trade, which could, and otherwise would, be more profitably employed, and as journalists in the interests of the public we must protest against it. It involves landowners and others in considerable expense and trouble in opposing such applications, and all to no purpose; for, even should the application be granted, the company have not a single shilling which properly belongs to them — they have consequently no capital, they have no credit, and they have no means to construct 96 miles of railway or any part thereof.
>
> The proper cause in such a case as this is to ascertain what can be sold of the undertaking. Wind up the concern, and thereby get rid of the Parliamentary agents, solicitors, engineers, and contractors of the scheme; blot it out from the map, and trust to time to blot out the memory of the unfortunate debenture holders, holders of Lloyd's bonds, and shareholders, the losses they have sustained and the misery they have endured by putting faith, trust, or confidence in what has turned out to be an utterly worthless concern.[22]

This was indeed savage criticism, but Dr Beattie and a handful of optimists on the Board showed no inclination to give up their scheme and, with their existing powers due to expire, the remaining promoters decided to obtain a further Act authorising completion of the line to Cockley Brake. At the same time, it was agreed that the financial structure of the company should be amended in the hope that creditors would take debenture stock in lieu of cash payments.

It was necessary, before proceeding with the Bill, for the company to arrange a special meeting, and this formality was carried out on 28th January, 1870. The meeting, held in the company office at 6 Victoria Street, Westminster, was poorly attended, and apart from Dr Beattie, the Secretary, and the company solicitor, only one shareholder bothered to turn up.

Opening the meeting, Dr Beattie apologised for the "unavoidable absence" of the Chairman, Lord Ernest Bruce. The solicitor was then asked to explain the Bill in the following terms:

> The Bill is for authorising an extension of the existing railway of the Midland Counties and South Wales to the Buckinghamshire, etc. as expressed in the notice of the meeting. It is to enable the Directors to raise money for the completion of the line to Banbury, and inasmuch as the powers for making that line have expired, it is proposed to authorise the construction of so much of the line as has not been completed. This Bill extends only to the extension of time for the construction of the company's line authorised by their Branch Act of 1865 and the Extension Act of 1865, and it is intended to propose that the time limited for making those railways should be read and have effect as if the passing of this Act had been mentioned in the original Act instead of the dates mentioned in those original Acts. It is proposed also that the capital of your Ross line, authorised by the Act of 1866, should be altogether separate capital from the other capital of the company.
>
> There are provisions in the Bill for restraining proceedings against the company,

to enable the Directors to complete the line without the interference of creditors, who at present have no claim upon it. There are also provisions for the issue of 'B' debenture stock, which is to be exchanged for the present mortgages upon the line and to be paid to other creditors. The Bill proposes also to alter the quorum of the Board; and that the holders of debenture stock should have the power of appointing Directors.

If this Bill passes as it stands, two Directors, to be called 'A' debenture Directors will be elected by the holders of that stock; and there will be the 'B' debenture Directors, and the Directors elected by the holders of the ordinary and preference shares. The quorum of the Directors will be three members; each class of Directors to retire annually to be determined by lot. The holders of debenture stocks of both classes have votes, and the holders of preference and ordinary shares are to have votes. Those are the general provisions of the Bill.

When the solicitor had finished explaining the Bill, Dr Beattie added a few words of his own. The solicitor had, he thought, explained the Bill so fully that there was little else to remark upon, but he reminded the small meeting that their existing powers would expire in the coming July, and it was absolutely necessary for a new application to Parliament to be made. It was, he said, vital that the line to Banbury should be finished because, unless it was completed, the Blockley line would never be carried out. The doctor added that it would also be necessary to repurchase the portion of line that had been sold by auction on 6th July, 1869. He then continued as follows:

> With these few remarks I beg to move that the Bill now submitted to this meeting, intitled 'A Bill for authorising an extension of the existing railway of the Midland Counties and South Wales to the Buckinghamshire, and for reviving the powers and extending the time for the purchase of land and construction of works authorised by former Acts of the company, and for suspending legal proceedings against the company, and for altering the financial arrangements of the company, and for other purposes' be . . . hereby approved, and the Directors are hereby authorised to proceed with the same, and to make or consent to such alterations and amendments therein during its further progress through Parliament as they may be advised are necessary or expedient.[23]

The motion was carried unanimously, and Dr Beattie closed the meeting by looking ahead to a time when the line could be extended beyond Banbury. Finally, with a hint of ironic humour, the Secretary suggested that the doctor was entitled to their thanks for chairing such a "great" meeting!

The 1870 Act

The Bill passed relatively smoothly through both houses, and on 14th July, 1870 *The Journal of the House of Commons* reported that it had received the Royal Assent.[24] The Act (33 & 34 Vic. cap. 122) authorised a line running from a point near Towcester to Cockley Brake, which was defined as:

> A railway eight miles, one furlong, one chain seventy five links in length, commencing from and out of the existing railway of the company at or near a field in the parish of Bradden in the county of Northampton numbered 10 in that parish on the deposited plans referred to in the company's Act of 1863, passing thence through or into the following parishes and places, or some of them (that is to say) Bradden Abthorpe, Slapton, Wappenham, Weedon-Lois, Falcott, Astwell, Helm-

AN

A C T

For authorising an Extension of the existing
Railway of the Midland Counties and South
Wales Railway Company to the Buckinghamshire Railway and for reviving the powers
and extending the time for purchase of Lands
and Construction of Works authorised by a
former Act of the Company and for suspend-
ing legal proceedings against the Company
and for altering the financial arrangements
of the Company and for other purposes.

[*Royal Assent* 14*th July* 1870.]

WHEREAS the Northampton and Banbury Junction Railway Com- Preamble.
pany now called the Midland Counties and South Wales Railway
Company and in this Act referred to as the Company were incorporated by The Northampton and Banbury Junction Railway Act 1863
5 (in this Act referred to as the Company's Act of 1863) and
were thereby authorised to make a railway from Blisworth to a junction
with the Banbury extension of the Buckinghamshire Railway (which
authorised railway is in this Act referred to as the Banbury Line) and
were thereby empowered to issue share capital of £140,000 in
10 14,000 shares of ten pounds each and to borrow on mortgage the sum
of £46,600:

The first page of the 1870 Act authorising the Extension to the N&BJR.

don, Stuchbury, Gretworth and Farthinghoe, all in the county of Northampton, and terminating in the said parish of Gretworth by a junction with the Banbury Extension of the Buckinghamshire Railway about five chains to the east of the bridge which carries the public road leading from Marston St. Lawrence to Farthinghoe over the said Banbury Extension near to a place called Cockley Brake.[25]

The financial provisions of the Act were more modest than those envisaged by the Directors in their original Bill, and whereas the Bill had sought powers to raise £500,000 worth of 'A' stock and £180,000 of 'B' stock, the Act provided for the creation of just £120,000 of 'A' stock and £180,000 of 'B' stock — the latter to be issued in exchange for the existing debentures and in payment to sundry creditors.

As far as the Board was concerned, the Act stipulated that two Directors should be elected by holders of 'A' stock, two more should be elected by holders of 'B' stock, and two Directors, to be called share Directors, would be elected by the holders of preference and ordinary shares.

A further provision empowered the company to seek compulsory purchase of "certain lands in the parish of Gayton in the county of Northampton, and also certain lands in the parish of Tiffield, in the same county", that had been "sold by auction on the 6th day of July, 1869 by order of the Court of Chancery". Another provision changed the name of the company from the Midland & Counties & South Wales Railway, back to the original, and more descriptive title of "Northampton & Banbury Junction Railway".

Construction Proceeds

Although the company's financial position remained precarious, the 1870 Act gave the Northampton & Banbury Junction supporters a breathing space in which to complete their original line, and it was reported, at the end of the year, that construction of the Towcester to Cockley Brake section had resumed, a contract for completion of the line to Cockley Brake having been awarded to the well-known contracting firm of John Aird & Son.

Leaving Towcester, the authorised route followed the Tove valley for about four miles. Beyond Astwell, however, westward progress was obstructed by an intervening ridge of higher land, and although a tributary stream of the Tove* provided a convenient path to Helmdon, the railway builders could not avoid a 1 in 65 climb in order to complete the line to Cockley Brake.

The line had originally been surveyed by Charles Liddell, a long-established engineer who had already carried out much engineering work on the Worcester & Hereford and other railways. Liddell is unlikely, however, to have spent much time on such a minor project as the N&BJR, and in reality, most of the initial surveys were probably undertaken by John Collister — who was, at one time, Joint Engineer of the Northampton & Banbury Junction Railway.

By the time that work had resumed in 1871, John Collister had been replaced as Resident Engineer by Edward Richards, who was, apparently, an associate (or pupil) of Charles Liddell, and shared his office at 24 Abingdon Street, Westminster. Liddell remained as a Joint Engineer with Richards, but there is no evidence to suggest that he exerted much influence during

* Some sources claim that this subsidiary channel is in fact the "main" stream.

construction of the Towcester to Cockley Brake line, and he is likely to have been retained merely as a consultant. However, Charles Liddell was one of the most famous engineers of his day, and there is no doubt that the presence of his name on N&BJR documents added an element of much-needed respectability to an otherwise ramshackle undertaking!

It is interesting to find that Edward Richards had also been responsible (with Charles Liddell) for the sixteen mile East Gloucestershire Railway between Witney and Fairford, which was being built at roughly the same time as the Northampton & Banbury Junction line. He also engineered the Ross & Monmouth and Halesowen & Bromyard lines — the connection with Ross being particularly significant in view of the proposed N&BJR extensions.

The works on the portion of line between Towcester and Banbury were being "rapidly proceeded with" during the early months of 1871, and on 31st August the delighted N&BJR shareholders were informed that the construction of their line "to the junction with the Banbury line of the London & North Western at Cockley Brake" had steadily progressed, and that the section from Towcester to Helmdon, a distance of 7½ miles, had already been opened for goods traffic, "thus making 11¾ miles open out of fifteen". From Helmdon to Cockley Brake the works were less advanced, but the state of the line "warranted the Directors in believing that the line would be opened throughout to Banbury in the early part of November".[26]

On 9th September, 1871 The Railway Times, having moderated its attitude towards the Northampton & Banbury Junction, was kind enough to print a relatively optimistic progress report:

> NORTHAMPTON & BANBURY JUNCTION . . . Up to 30th June last the Directors had issued 'B' debenture stock to the amount of £162,738 in settlement of debentures and other outstanding liabilities to a like amount. They had succeeded in effecting an equitable settlement of all questions between the company and the inspectors of the former contractor, and the deeds carrying those arrangements into effect had been completed. The whole of the 'A' debenture stock had been placed.
>
> The receipts on the 4½ miles from Blisworth to Towcester during the past half-year had shown a steady increase. The gross receipts after allowing for the coal traffic . . . showed an average of about £18 per mile per week. The receipts for the half-year on the 4½ miles amounted to £1,434, and for the corresponding period last year to £1,242, showing an increase of £142.
>
> The report of Mr E. Richards, the Engineer, stated that the passenger station at Blisworth for the joint use of the company and the London & North Western was completed, and the other station buildings on the line were in an advanced state.[27]

In theory, the company's creditors should have been satisfied with these encouraging developments, which suggested that, as a modest branch line, the N&BJR might at least break even. Dr Beattie, on the other hand, refused to abandon his grand scheme for a trunk line to South Wales, and in February 1871 there had been an attempt to revive the Ross-on-Wye extension project. To further this aim, the Directors proposed to raise no less than £1,019,000 by shares and debenture issues, and in view of the revival of N&BJR fortunes implicit in this scheme, it was proposed that the company's name be changed back to the impressive-sounding Midland Counties & South Wales Railway.

It was, however, difficult for Dr Beattie and the other expansionists to convince the reconstituted Board that such schemes were in any way feasible, and having allowed their many creditors to have a say in N&BJR affairs, the original Directors and their supporters were unable to achieve their long-standing ambitions. In February 1872, for instance, there was a proposal that the line might be extended eastwards to Northampton, to "enable the pas-.sengers to proceed from Blisworth to Northampton without the inconvenience of changing".

In retrospect, the Northampton proposal was eminently sensible, in that it would have allowed the N&BJR to reach a large centre of population independently of the London & North Western. Unfortunately, the scheme was vociferously opposed by a Mr McKenzie, who turned up at the company's February meeting claiming to represent the wishes of "a large number of shareholders".[28] Interestingly, Mr McKenzie was particularly concerned about any veiled ambitions on the part of the Midland Railway, and he proposed that any Bill to promote lines to Northampton should have special clauses to "limit the power of the Midland", and this motion was carried by a show of hands.[29]

Opening to Cockley Brake Junction

Meanwhile, John Aird & Son had made good progress with the Towcester to Cockley Brake line, and having passed its Board of Trade inspection, the railway was opened to traffic on 1st June, 1872.

The completed railway traversed an area of rolling, Cotswold-like hills, and its civil engineering features were relatively heavy. There was, for example, a deep cutting between Slapton and Wappenham, while, further west, the line descended towards its junction with the LNWR on a great curving embankment. There were several overbridges, together with one or two small underbridges where streams or farm tracks passed under the line. The intermediate stations at Helmdon and Wappenham had buildings and track layouts recalling those on other lines engineered by Edward Richards, and the trackbed was wide enough to accommodate a second line of rails in the event of doubling being carried out.

There was no station at Cockley Brake, the idea being that Northampton & Banbury Junction trains would continue westwards, along the LNWR line, to Banbury. In general, the new line was well-built, and its attractive stations were a credit to the financially-embarrassed N&BJR — which might have been tempted to erect some form of makeshift wooden stations instead of the solid, yet simple brick structures that were in fact provided.

From an operational viewpoint the worst feature of the line was its gradients; the route climbed relentlessly towards Helmdon summit, the steepest sections being a stretch of 1 in 65, followed immediately by a descent of 1 in 70 on the approach to Cockley Brake. It would, perhaps, be churlish to criticise this point too severely, for after all, the alternative to these gradients would have been an extremely costly tunnel. What really mattered, in 1872, was that the Northampton & Banbury Junction Railway was at last complete, and mechanical communication had finally reached hitherto remote rural communities such as Slapton, Abthorpe and Wappenham.

Sources for Chapter Two

19. Northampton & Banbury Junction Act 1866 (29 & 30 Vic. cap. 310).
20. *The Worcester Herald*, 10th May, 1862.
21. *The Times*, 5th July, 1869.
22. *The Railway Times*, 24th July, 1869, pps. 723–24.
23. *loc.cit.* 29th July, 1870, p. 102.
24. *The Journal of the House of Commons*, 14th July, 1870.
25. Northampton & Banbury Junction Act 1870 (33 & 34 Vic. cap. 122).
26. Northampton & Banbury Junction Half-Year Report, August 1871.
27. *The Railway Times*, 9th September, 1871, p. 869.
28. *The Railway Times*, 10th February, 1872, p. 148.
29. *Ibid.*

245.—NORTHAMPTON AND BANBURY JUNCTION.

Incorporated by 26 and 27 Vic., cap. 220 (28th July, 1863), to construct a line from Blisworth to Farthinghoe. Capital, 140,000*l.* in 10*l.* shares; loans, 46,600*l.* Debentures converted into B debenture stock by Act of 1870.

By 28 and 29 Vic., cap. 361, Northampton and Banbury (Branch) Act, 1865, the company were empowered to make a branch line to connect their railway with the Northampton and Peterborough line of the London and North Western, and to raise additional capital to the extent of 193,300*l.*, viz.:—By shares, 145,000*l.*; on loan, 48,200*l.* Debentures converted into B debenture stock by Act of 1870. Power to enter into traffic arrangements with Great Western. An agreement is scheduled to this Act by which the company obtains running powers over the Buckinghamshire line of the London and North Western, from Cockley Brake to Banbury, with use of the London and North Western and Great Western Stations.

By 28 and 29 Vic., cap 362 Northampton and Banbury Railway (Extensions) Act, 1865, the company were empowered to extend their railway to Chipping Norton and Blockley, and to raise additional capital to the extent of 666,600*l.*, viz.:—By shares, 500,000*l.*; on loan 116,600*l.*, but by the Act of 1870 these borrowing powers were cancelled

By 29 and 30 Vic., cap. 310, Northampton and Banbury Act, 1866, the company were empowered to extend their railway from Blockley to Ross, and to raise additional capital to the extent of 733,000*l.*, viz.:—By shares, 550,000*l.*; on loan, 183,000*l.*, but by the Act of 1870 these borrowing powers were cancelled. By this Act the company obtain running powers over the Midland, between Bickford and Tewkesbury, over the Ross and Monmouth, and over the Worcester Dean Forest and Monmouth, between Newport and Monmouth. The name of the company was changed from the Northampton and Banbury Junction to the Midland Counties and South Wales. Total length of line authorised, 96½ miles.

The portion of the railway from Blisworth to Towcester, 4 miles, was opened for traffic in April, 1866.

By 33 and 34 Vic., cap. 122 (14th July, 1870), the company resumed its original name of Northampton and Banbury Junction Railway Company, and was authorised to make the line from Bradden to Banbury in substitution of the railway, the powers for which were granted in 1863, but had lapsed, and for purchasing the necessary land. It also revived the powers of the Branch Act, 1865, and contained provisions for raising 120,000*l.* of A debenture stock for finishing the line to Banbury, and paying for land, and 180,000*l.* of B debenture stock, to be issued in exchange for the existing debentures, and in payment of the general creditors. The works on the line between Towcester and Banbury are being rapidly proceeded with.

Meetings in February and August.

No. of Directors (as settled by Act of 1870) 6, viz.:—2 elected by A debenture stockholders; 2 by B debenture stockholders; and 2 by shareholders; quorum, 3. *Qualification*, 500*l.* of the respective stocks.

DIRECTORS:

Chairman—The Right Hon. LORD ERNEST BRUCE, M.P., 6, St. George's Place, S.W.
Deputy-Chairman—ALEXANDER BEATTIE, Esq., M.D., 45, Porchester Terrace, Hyde Park, W.

Robert Amadeus Heath, Esq., 31, Old Jewry, E.C.
Walter Amos Michael, Esq., 60, Threadneedle Street, E.C.
Lachlan Mackintosh Rate, Esq. King's Arms Yard, E.C.
Henry James Sheldon, Esq., Brailes House, Shipston-on-Stour, Warwickshire.

OFFICERS.—Sec. and Gen. Man., J. Wilson Theobald, 6, Victoria Street, S.W.; Traff. Supt., J. B. Crabtree, Towcester; Engs., Charles Liddell, C.E., and Edward Richards, C.E., 24, Abingdon Street, Westminster, S.W.; Solicitors, Bircham and Co., 7, Parliament Street, Westminster, S.W.

Offices—6, Victoria Street, Westminster, S.W., and Towcester Station, Northamptonshire.

Extract from the 1871 Bradshaw's Shareholders' Manual.

Towcester station looking east towards Blisworth in the early 1900s. This turn-of-the-century view is of particular interest in that it shows the engine shed (partially visible beyond the canopy). Note also the platelayer's velocipede on the track.

Lens of Sutton

Chapter Three

Nineteenth Century Developments (1872–1900)

The newly-opened Northampton & Banbury Junction line settled down to eke out an impecunious existence as a minor cross-country link between Blisworth and Banbury. Despite its independent status, the line was little more than a branch of the London & North Western, and moreover, its isolated eastern terminus at Blisworth served no places of importance. If trains could have exercised running powers over the LNWR to Northampton, the line would have formed a useful link between two relatively important urban centres, but in reality, few people wished to travel from Banbury to Blisworth or vice versa, and in these circumstances the N&BJ line was unable to attract significant passenger or freight traffic.

The East & West Junction Railway

There remained a possibility that the original section of line might be extended beyond its existing limits to reach Chipping Norton or some other destination, and although the N&BJ company's own extension schemes were unsuccessful, the Northampton & Banbury Junction shareholders were heartened by the activities of a neighbouring company known as The East & West Junction Railway.

The East & West Junction had obtained its Act on 23rd June, 1864 (27 & 28 Vic. cap. 76), and the ambitious E&WJR promoters were thereby authorised to begin construction of a 33½ mile line from Towcester, on the Northampton & Banbury Junction, to Old Stratford, on the Honeybourne branch of the Great Western Railway. The East & West Junction had an authorised capital of £300,000 in £20 shares, together with borrowing powers for another £200,000; its Chairman was Sir Cusack Roney, and the Directors included (in 1864) Sir Charles Mordant MP, Mathew Malcolm and William John Addison.[30]

Construction work commenced at Towcester on 3rd August, 1864, the first sod being cut by Lady Palmerston. Sadly, the East & West Junction scheme was badly hit by the economic crisis of 1866, and despite a further Act authorising additional share capital of £300,000 and loans of £100,000, the promoters were forced to abandon their scheme through lack of money.

It seemed that the Towcester to Stratford-upon-Avon line would never be completed, but, eventually, improved trading conditions enabled the promoters to revive their original project, and in 1869 an agreement made with the company's creditors allowed construction to resume. It was hoped that the line could be completed for £230,000 within a time limit of 2 years, and in an atmosphere of renewed optimism, the first section of line was opened from Fenny Compton to Kineton on 1st June, 1871.

In 1871 the East & West Junction Railway obtained an extension of time to complete its works, and two years later, on 1st July, 1873 the line was completed throughout from Kineton to Stratford-upon-Avon, and from Fenny Compton to Towcester. The new line actually joined the Northampton & Banbury Junction Railway at Greens Norton Junction, to the west of Towcester, but East & West Junction trains were able to run through to Blisworth (having secured running powers over the N&BJR).

33

In theory the Northampton & Banbury Junction supporters should have welcomed the East & West Junction with open arms, but in reality the attitude of the N&BJR was, at first, highly ambiguous. Indeed, a major row had developed as early as 1865 when, without properly consulting the Northampton & Banbury Junction Directors, the East & West Junction promoters had made a public announcement concerning running powers over the N&BJR and a crossing of the London & North Western at Blisworth. This was, to say the least, a matter of extreme sensitivity, and in December 1865 the Northampton & Banbury Junction Directors called a special meeting to discuss the matter. Dr Beattie referred, somewhat dismissively, to a "proposed line called the East & West Junction Railway"; this new company had, he claimed, issued a prospectus which conveyed "an erroneous impression" regarding running powers, and the N&BJR Secretary was instructed to write to the press so that the alleged errors could be publicly corrected.[31]

The reasons for Dr Beattie's extreme annoyance were probably threefold: first, the East & West Junction had apparently acted without fully consulting the N&BJR; second, the N&BJR was itself desirous of achieving proper running powers over the antipathetic LNWR at Blisworth; and third, the East & West Junction may have been seen as a potential rival.

To understand this last point, it is necessary to remember that Dr Beattie and his fellow-N&BJR Directors hoped to build a major trunk route between Northamptonshire and South Wales, but, at a time when these ambitions seemed attainable, the East & West Junction was itself promoting a series of grandiose extensions. In 1866 for instance, the E&WJR contemplated an extension from Towcester, through Stony Stratford, to the Great Northern Railway at Hitchin. The projected line would have been 37 miles 52 chains in length, and it would have incorporated junctions with the Midland Railway and the LNWR. Another, much shorter line, would have joined the Southam Railway at Sheepford Bridge, but more worrying, for the N&BJR, was the thought that the East & West Junction might also extend *westwards*, in open competition with the proposed Banbury to Ross-on-Wye line.

In the event, the East & West Junction Railway suffered as badly as the N&BJR in the 1866 financial crisis, and in January 1875 the E&WJR went into receivership. If anything, the East & West Junction Railway was in an even worse predicament as the Northampton & Banbury Junction, and on 31st July, 1877 its passenger services were suspended, leaving the bankrupt company as a goods-only line with a residual service of freight trains on its near-derelict system.

The cessation of East & West Junction passenger services must have been a great disappointment, not only for the E&WJR shareholders, but also for the N&BJR, which lost revenue on the line from Blisworth to Towcester. Indeed, Northampton & Banbury Junction receipts had looked quite healthy when the E&WJR was in full operation, having risen from about £3000 a year in the early 1870s to no less than £9000 a year in 1874/75. In the half-year ending 31st December, 1874, for example, the N&BJR earned £5270, while in the six months to 30th June, 1875 the railway earned a further £4272 (comparing favourably with just £1434 over the corresponding six months from January to June 1870.[32]

Sadly, the Northampton & Banbury Junction company was so burdened by debt that any operating profit was rapidly subsumed; thus, expenses of £4473 for the six months ending 31st December, 1874 left only £797 to be carried forward, and in the next half-year expenses of £4417 resulted in a loss of £145.[33]

N&BJR Motive Power

Faced with mounting expenses, the Northampton & Banbury Junction Railway was hard-pressed to maintain its small fleet of hired engines, but — perhaps for reasons of status — the company spent £1475 on a second-hand 0–6–0 in December 1872. Built by Tayleur & Co. in 1855, the engine involved in this deal had originally been South Staffordshire Railway No. 21 *Ajax*; it subsequently passed to the LNWR, becoming No. 1827 in that company's fleet. The engine had 5 ft coupled wheels and 17 in. × 24 in. cylinders. Two more locomotives were purchased from the LNWR in the following year. One of these was an 0–4–2T with 5 ft coupled wheels and 16 in. × 24 in. cylinders, while the other was an 0–6–0 tender engine with 5 ft wheels and 18 in. × 24 in. cylinders. The tank engine had been constructed by Sharp Brothers, and carried the LNWR number 1831, while its companion was a veteran Hawthorn goods engine, dating from 1848 and carrying the LNWR number 1849.[34]

For a time, the company struggled on with these second-hand machines, but in August 1875 it was reported that, the "locomotive power of the railway having been found insufficient", a new arrangement had been made with the London & North Western whereby that company would supply "such locomotive power as may be required at a fixed charge of 1 shilling per train per mile".[35] This agreement was, apparently, a retrospective deal that had come into effect on 1st March, 1875 (suggesting that the N&BJR had faced a locomotive crisis at that time, and had called upon the North Western for emergency help.

19th Century Train Services

Northampton & Banbury Junction train services were modest in the extreme and the basic branch timetable provided no more than 3–4 workings each way between Blisworth and Banbury (LNWR). In 1888, for example, daily operations began with the departure of the 7.30 am "Parliamentary" from Banbury, and this morning up working reached Blisworth at 8.37, having taken 67 minutes to accomplish its 20½ mile journey through rural Northamptonshire. At 9.05 am the train returned to Banbury, arriving at 10.18, in good time to form the 10.25 up service to Blisworth. A further down working left Blisworth at 12.55 pm, but this service ran only as far as Towcester (apart from Thursdays, when it continued through to Banbury as a "market" train). The next down service departed from Blisworth at 4.38 pm, and there was a balancing up working from Banbury at 6.05 pm which reached Blisworth at 7.07. An additional up train left Banbury at 3.18 pm on Thursdays only, and there was a short distance evening service from Blisworth to Towcester at 8.08 pm.

Study of these timings suggests that at least two locomotives and train sets were needed to work the daily branch timetable, and (remembering that Northampton & Banbury Junction train services were worked by the LNWR after 1875–76), it seems reasonable to conclude that Blisworth services were integrated with those on the Banbury to Verney Junction line. Thus, the 7.30 am up train to Blisworth is likely to have been worked by a train that had previously worked a Banbury to Verney Junction diagram (alternatively, the 4.38 pm from Blisworth to Banbury may have remained at Banbury overnight prior to forming the following day's 7.30 am departure; if this was indeed the case, stock from the Banbury to Bletchley line would have been available to form the 6.05 pm evening departure for Blisworth).

A curious feature of the 1888 timetable concerns the intermediate LNWR station at Farthinghoe, which was served by both Northampton & Banbury and North Western services. However, Blisworth to Banbury trains called in the down direction to set-down only, and passengers were not supposed to use these services for short distance journeys between Farthinghoe and Banbury. A similar situation applied in the up direction, in which case Northampton & Banbury Junction trains called to pick-up only. One assumes that these restrictions were imposed by the LNWR to ensure that as much traffic as possible was conveyed by ordinary North Western services between Banbury and Verney Junction.

In addition to the "main" Northampton & Banbury Junction services between Blisworth and Banbury, the Blisworth to Towcester section was also served by East & West Junction trains en route from Blisworth to Stratford-upon-Avon, and in the early 1870s this section of the N&BJ carried 2 up and 2 down East & West Junction trains. Interestingly, these services conveyed through coaches for London Euston after 1873 — giving Towcester residents a useful link with the metropolis. As we have seen the East & West Junction Railway was forced to abandon its meagre passenger services in 1877, but when the Blisworth to Stratford-upon-Avon service was eventually resumed in 1885 the company provided a slightly improved timetable of three trains in each direction.

A further development took place in 1890 when the East & West Junction Railway introduced a programme of special Saturdays-only through trains known as the 'Shakespeare Specials'. Designed to attract weekend leisure travellers who might otherwise have used the rival Great Western route to Stratford-upon-Avon, the 'Shakespeare Specials' offered prospective customers an attractive package of cheap fares and admission tickets to selected tourist attractions. Unfortunately, the track layout at Blisworth did not easily permit through running from the LNWR and what might, from the North Western's point of view, have been a lucrative "holiday" route to Stratford, was compromised by the time spent shunting trains from one system to the other at Blisworth. A further complication stemmed from the East & West Junction company's use of Westinghouse air brakes instead of the vacuum brakes favoured by other lines, and for this reason the 'Shakespeare Specials' were initially worked throughout by London & North Western Railway locomotives. (Later, a few E&W engines were equipped with vacuum brakes, and thereafter the excursions changed locomotives at Blisworth.)

Banbury and Northampton.—N. and B. Junction.

STATIONS.	a.m.	a.m.	p.m.	THURSDAYS ONLY.	p.m.	STATIONS.	a.m.	a.m.		noon	p.m.
BANBURY ..	7 30	10 25	3†18		6 5	Liverpool	2 35	7 20	...	12 0	4 5
Farthinghoe* ..	7*37	10*32	3*25		6"12	Manchester	...	7 45	...	12 0	4 15
Helmdon	7 52	10 47	3†47		6 27	Birmingham ..	7 30	9 40	...	2 10	6 15
Wappenham ..	8 4	10 59	3†54		6 39	London (Eustn.)	7 15	11 0	...	3 0	6 30
Towcester	8 22	11 15	4 10		6 52	Welton	8 39	10 10	...	2 30	...
Blisworth	8 37	11 30	4 25		7 7	Weedon	8 50	10 23		2 43	...
Northampton .	8 55	11 45	4 50		7 25	Northampton .	8 45	12 30	DAYS ONLY.	4 20	7 50
Weedon	9 9	1 2	4 49	...	8 17	Blisworth......	9 5	12 55		4 38	8 8
Welton	9 22	1 16	5 2	...	8 32	Towcester......	9 24	1 10		4 53	8 23
London (Eustn.)	10 45	2 45	7 10	...	10 15	Wappenham ..	9 40	1†25		5 6	...
Birmingham ..	10 40	2 0	6 40	...	9 35	Helmdon	9 53	1†37		5 18	...
Manchester	12 30	4 20	8 20	...	11 20	Farthinghoe‡ ..	10‡ 8	...		5 37	...
Liverpool	12 40	4 40	8 40	...	12 0	BANBURY ..	10 18	2† 0		5 45	...

* Calls at Farthinghoe to pick up only.   ‡ Calls to set down only.

Passenger timetable for 1888, as published in Local Guide.

NORTHAMPTON, BLISWORTH, DAVENTRY & BANBURY.

WEEK DAYS.	a.m.	a.m.	a.m.	a.m.	a.m.	WS	a.m.	noon	p.m.	p.m.		p.m.	p.m.	p.m.	p.m.	p.m.	p.m.	p.m.	p.m.	a.m.
NORTHAMPTON ...dep	6 25	7 35	8 80	...	10 10	10 45	11 5	12 55	1 80	2 5	...	4 5	6 20	...	6 55	7 55	8 45	...		10 40
Blisworth ....arr	6 85	7 44	8 40	.	10 20	10 55	11 13	1 5	1 40	2 15	...	4 15	6 30	.	7 5	8 5	8 55	.		11C18
Weedon ....arr	...	.	8 55	.	10 55	11 10	...	1 25	...	2 35	...	4 35	6 47	...	7 22	...	...	.		11 32
DAVENTRY ,,	...	.	9 20	.	11;10	11 22	...	1 52	...	.	...	5 20	7 0	...	8 0	...	.			
			a.m.					a.m.	a.m.	noon		p.m.			p.m.					
London (Euston) ......dep	...	.	7 15	...	...	9I30	10 10	...	12 15	...	2 45	...	5 0	5 0	...	7I 0			
Liverpool (Lime St.) ,,	...	.	2 85	.	...	...	7 40	...	9 45	...	12I 0	...	2 0	2 0	...	5I10			
Manchester (Lon. Rd.),,	...	.	12 0	.	...	...	8 30	...	10 0	...	12I 0	...	2 10	2 10	...	5I30			
Birmingham (New St.),,	...	.	7 80	.	...	...	8 45	10I0	11 50	...	2I 0	...	5 0	...	7I 0			
Rugby ,,	...	.	8 19	8 25	...	10 15	10 58	...	1 12	...	3I 8	...	5 30	5 30	...	8I12			
Blisworth ....dep	...	.	8 55	9 10		11 18	1 10	...	2 40	...	4 80	4S45	6 87	7 22	...	8S 57			
Towcester ....arr	...	.	...	9 25	...	11 33	1 25	...	2 57	...	4 45	...	6 53	7 37	...	9S 12			
Stratford-on-Avon ...arr (E. & W. Junc. Ry.)	...	.	10 22	.		12 43	...	4 7	...	...	6 S6	...	8 0	...	10S17			
Wappenham.............,,	...	.	...	9 38	.		1 33	...	...	4 58	...		7 50	...			
Helmdon ....,,	...	.	...	9 48	.		1 50	...	...	5 10	...		8 2	...			
Farthinghoe ....,,	...	.	...	10 8	.		2 5	...	...	5 23	...		8 19	...			
BANBURY ....,,	...	.	...	10 18	.		2 15	...	...	5 33	...		8 30	...			

	a.m.	a.m.	a.m.		a.m.		a.m.	a.m.		p.m.		p.m.			p.m.	p.m.	p.m.	p.m.		a.m.	p.m.
BANBURY ....dep	.	.	7 25	...	.	...	10 45	...	...	...	...	3 12	...	6 5	...						
Farthinghoe ....,,	.	Mon. only.	7 32	.	.	...	10 52	...	...	...	3 19	...	6 12	...						
Helmdon ....,,	.		7 47	.	.	...	11 7	...	...	...	3 35	...	6 26	...						
Wappenham ....,,	.		7 59	.	.	...	11 19	...	...	...	3 47	...	6 38	...						
E. & W. Junc Ry.)																				
Stratford-on-Avon ...dep	.	7 5	...	8 52	...	11 40	...	...	...	3 10	...	6 55	...						
Towcester ....dep	.		8 15	...	10 0	.	11 85	12 50	...	...	4 0	...	6 52	8 2	...					
Blisworth ....arr	.	8 21	8 30	...	10 15	.	11 50	1 5	...	...	4 15	4 30	7 7	8 17	...					
Rugby ....arr	.	9 30	9 30	...	11 0	.	1 I35	2 I12	...	...	4 55	6 47	7 52	9 42	...					
Birmingham (New St.) ,,	.	10 25	10 35	...	11 50	.	2 45	3 47	...	...	6 35	7I 5	9 50	11I50	...					
Manchester (Lon. Rd.) ,,	.	14 45	12 45	.	2 30		4 20	5 16	...	...	8 15	9 55	...	1§ 5	...					
Liverpool (Lime St.) ,,	.	2 5	2 5	.	2 5		...	5 0	...	...	8 40	10 10	...	12§40	...					
London (Euston) ......,,	.	10 10	10 10	.	12 10		...	2 40	...	...	6I35	...	10I15	...					
DAVENTRY ....dep	.		8 15		9 55	10I 0	...	12 85	...	...	4 15	5 40	...	7 5	...					
Weedon ....,,	.		8 50		10 6	10 15	...	12 45	1 84	...	4 26	5 56	...	7 46	...			10 31	3 7		
Blisworth ....dep	6 45		9 5		10 30	10 40	11 85	11 55	1 15	1 50	...	2 30	...	4 40	6 37	7 15	8 25	9 53		10C46	3C21
NORTHAMPTON .....arr	6 53		9 14		10 30	10 50	11 35	12 5	1 25	2 0	...	2 40	...	4 40	6 47	7 25	8 34	10 3		11 25	3 47

Parliamentary Tickets are issued to and from the Banbury Line by the 7.40 a.m. from Banbury, and the 8.30 a.m. from Northampton.
WS—Wednesdays and Saturdays only.

†—Wednesdays and Saturdays excepted.
‖—Via Weedon
§—Arrives Manchester 2.55 a.m., and Liverpool 3.0 a.m. on Sundays.

C—Via Roade.
I—Via Northampton.
For particulars of Through Carriages see page 138.

S—Saturdays only

LNWR passenger timetable for December 1894.

The first Newspaper stamp issued by the Company.

NORTHAMPTON and BLISWORTH.—London and North Western.

	Down.								Week Days.									Sundays.		
Miles	Castle Station,	mrn	mrn	mrn	mrn	mrn	aft	aft	aft	aft	aft	aft	aft	aft	aft		aft	mrn	Via	mrn
	Northampton ...dep.	1ʏ20	7 15	8 20	8 50	9 55	1030	1215	10 1	30 1	45	4 5	4 25	5 20	0 7	5 7 35		1153	1 20	Roade.	1050
4¼	Blisworth 442 ...arr.	1ʏ30	7 23	8 28	8 58	10 5	1038	1223	1	18 1	38 1	53	4 15	5 4	33 5	30 6	8 7 15 7 45		1143	1 30		1119

Mls	Up.	mrn	mrn	mrn	mrn	mrn	aft	aft	aft	aft	aft	aft	aft	aft	aft		Via	mrn
—	Blisworth ....dep	8 53	9 15	1020	1035	11 0	1145	1	48	2 10	3 18	4	47	6 0	7 30	8 0 9 0		Roade.	1038 3 23
4¼	Northampton (Castle) arr.	9 2	9 23	1030	1048	11 8	1155	1	58	2 20	3 28	4	55	6 8	7 41	8 10 9 10			1125 3 55

p Except Mondays. *s* Saturdays only.

BLISWORTH, TOWCESTER, and BANBURY.—Northampton and Banbury Junction.
Traffic Supt.. E. Stanton, Blisworth.   Sec.. W. Leigh-Hunt, London.

	Down.		Week Days.					Up.		Week Days.		
Miles from Blisworth	Euston Station,	gov	mrn	aft	aft		Miles	Merton Street Station,	gov	mrn	aft	aft
	404London ......dep	7 10	o1010	2 45	6 z 5			Banbury.........dep.	7 25	7 25	1030	3 12	6 7
	412Lʏroor.(Lime St.)..	2635	7 15	12o0	2 0		4	Farthinghoe...........	7 32	7 32	1037	3 19	6 7
	NORTHMPTN (Catle)	8 50	12 15	4 25	7 5		8½	Helmdon	7 47	7 50	1051	3 40	6 24
—	Blisworth ......dep	9 14	12 30	4 40	7 24		12¼	Wappenham	7 59	4 11	13 52	6 34
4½	Towcester	9 27	12 42	4 52	7 37		16	Towcester 443	8 12	8 20	1124	8	6 50
8½	Wappenham	9 38	12 54	5 17	50		20¼	Blisworth 404, 413 arr.	8 25	8 35	1126	4 20	7 3
12	Helmdon	9 48	1 4	5 10	8 2		25½	NORTHMPTN (Catle) ar 9 5 2	9 2	1155	4 55	7 41
16½	Farthinghoe 440	10 3	1 19	5 23	8 19		150¼	405Lʏroot. (LimeSt.).	1055	1 35	o 88 50	A1240
20¼	Banbury ‖ 74, 81, 98 arr	1013	1 28	5 33	8 27		80¾	413London (Euston).	1050	1140	5 6 0	9 50

b Except Wednesdays and Saturdays.   *k* Arrives at 3 10 mrn. on Sundays ; 1st and 3rd class.
o Via Northampton (Castle).   *z* By slip carriage.   *l* Merton Street Station.
☞ For **OTHER TRAINS** between Blisworth and Towcester, see page 442.

Bradshaw's passenger timetable for April 1910.

BLISWORTH, TOWCESTER, BANBURY, WOODFORD, STRATFORD-ON-AVON, & BROOM JUNCTION,—(1st and 3rd class).
Stratford-upon-Avon and Midland Junction.
Offices—Stratford-on-Avon.   Man. and Eng., Russell Willmott.   Sec. and Acct., A. E. Diggins.

	Down.			Week Days only.							Up.		Week Days only.				
	Euston Station,	mrn		mrn	aft	aft	aft	aft	aft			590CHELTENHAM‡..dep			mrn	mrn	aft	aft	aft
	414London ......dep	7 10		9ʏ20	1215	2 45	4ꟻ30	6ɡ5	10ꟻ0			Broom Junction...dep	8 15		9 24	1 27		4 45
	450NORTHAMPTN(C.)	8 50		1050	1 45	4 22	6 0	7 5	1133		1½	Bidford-on-Avon	8 20		11 10	2 42		6 20
4	Blisworth ......dep	9 13		1056	2 10	4 50	6 17	7 30	1150		7½	Binton	8 30		11 22	2 55		6 33
	Towcester ...... arr	9 21		1058	2 18	4 58	6 25	7 38	12 0		8½	Stratford - on - ꟻ arr	8 35		11 30			6 40
—	Towcester ......dep	9 14			2ꟻ35	0		7 40			—	Avon‡106,107 ‖ dep	8 40		12 35		4 30	6 30
12	Wappenham	9 39			2ꟻ45	9		7 48			12	Ettington	8 12		12 46		4 40	6 40
16¼	Farthinghoe 448	9 59			3ꟻ5			7 56			18½	Kineton	8 21		12 54		4 50	6 49
20¼	Banbury ‖ 80, 84 arr.	10 6			3 15	56		8 14			23½	Fenny Compton 80, 84.	8 33		1 5		5 1	8 1
—	Towcester ..... dep	9 24				6 39					30	Byfield	8 44		1 16		5 14	6 58
4½	Blakesley	9 33				6 35					32	Byfield .... dep	8 48	9 51	1 18		5 16	6 58
11	Merton Pinkney	9 41				6 42					32	Woodford *655.. arr	8 52	9 53	1 22		5 18 6 57	8 18
13¼	Byfield ...... arr.	9 48				6 49					101	655London(M'lebone) a	1026	1155	3 0		6 43 8 43	9 55
17¼	Byfield .... dep	9 51				6 53					—	Woodford *....dep	9 18				Stop
	Woodford *648.. arr.	9 58				6 57					—	Byfield .... arr.	9 23			
—	448London(M'lebone)d 6 45		8 45	1215		450 6ꟻ20				—	Byfield ....dep						5 18
—	Woodford * ....dep	9 18		1030	1 59	4 59	6 19 7 45				34½	Merton Pinkney	9 42				5 26
—	Byfield .... arr	9 22		1034	2 3		6 47 48				37	Blakesley	9 48				5 32
—	Byfield ....dep			1037	2 7		6 167 50				41½	Towcester ...... arr.	9 55				5 39	aft
33	Fenny Compton 80, 84. Stop			1046	2 18		6 278 1				Mls	Banbury ‖ 80, 84...	7 25		1040		3635	6 2
29	Kineton			1059	2 28		6 38 8 12				4	Farthinghoe	7 34		1048		3644	6 10
33	Ettington			11 7	2 37		6 468 20				8½	Helmdon	7 47		1058		3655	6 22
38¼	Stratford - on - ꟻ mrn			1116	2 46		6 558 29				12¼	Wappenham	7 58		11 6		464	6 32
42	Avon‡106,107 ‖ dep 7 35		1031	2 53							16½	Towcester...... arr.	8 7		1113		4ꟻ13	6 39
44½	Binton	7 43		1039	2 58 48						—	Towcester ...450 dep	8 10 10 0		1115	1 25	4 155 41	6 50
45½	Bidford-on-Avon	7 51		1047	2 16 5 58						4	Blisworth 414, 423, arr	8 20 1010		1125	1 35	4 25 5 51	7 0
49½	Broom Junc. 583.. arr	7 55		1051	2 29 6 0						50	450NORTHAMPTN(C.) ar	9 3 1050		1155	2 1	5 0 8 87	45
70½	585CHELTENHAM‡. arr	9 25		1213	4 37 56						1068	413London (Euston) ar	1010 12 0		1ꟻ5	4 1	6 0 8 25	9 50

A Through Carriage to London (Marylebone).   B By Through Slip Carriage to Stratford-on-Avon.   h Through Carriage to Stratford-on-Avon.   † S. M. J. Station, 1 mile from G. W. Station.
b Thursdays only.   F Via Northampton.   * Woodford and Hinton.   1 Queen's Road, Lansdown.
g By Slip Carriage.   ‖ Merton Street.
☞ For **OTHER TRAINS** between Farthinghoe and Banbury, see page 448.

Bradshaw's passenger timetable for October 1911.

The second issue Newspaper stamp issued by the Company.

The Northampton & Banbury Junction line served a predominately agricultural district with no large scale industries, and for this reason freight traffic was rarely important. The principal sources of traffic were coal inwards and farm product outwards, and such freight was usually conveyed by "mixed" trains. Officially, only seven goods vehicles were allowed to be hauled by each train, but this rule was relaxed in the case of cattle traffic — up to ten cattle wagons being permitted on passenger workings.

The through 'Shakespeare Specials' were clearly a highlight of normal summer operation, but it is interesting to recall that, once a year, the somnolent pace of everyday life was transformed by the Grafton Hunt Steeplechases which were held at Towcester on Easter Monday. In connection with this event, the Northampton & Banbury Junction line was called upon to handle a variety of through excursion trains from "foreign" stations, the usual practice being for incoming trains to arrive from both Banbury and Blisworth. Several thousand extra passengers arrived in the morning and departed in the evening, and on these occasions the LNWR helped out by providing additional coaching stock; many of the vehicles involved were London suburban sets, while (in later years at least) others were from the North London line. On arrival at Towcester, the race trains were stabled in the goods yard, and the visiting engines were then sent light to Blisworth for turning (later, the installation of a turntable at Towcester obviated these inconvenient light engine movements).

Further Extension Schemes

Although the Towcester races brought welcome additional traffic to the line at Easter, they could not sustain the line throughout the rest of the year, and for this reason the Northampton & Banbury Directors welcomed the formation of the Easton Neston Mineral & Towcester, Roade & Olney Junction Railway in 1879. Authorised by an Act of 15th August, 1879, this ponderously-named organisation hoped to build a 10½ mile connecting line between Towcester and the Midland-owned Bedford & Northampton Railway at Ravenstone Wood, near Olney. There were also thoughts of a link to the LNWR at Roade, but from the Northampton & Banbury Junction's point of view the proposed link to the Midland was of much greater significance. If successfully completed, this new line would bring the Midland into the area, while at the same time lessening the N&BJ company's dependence on the London & North Western Railway.[36]

Further west, a separate company known as the Evesham Redditch & Stratford-upon-Avon Junction Railway had been formed on 5th August, 1873, and when opened to traffic on 2nd June, 1879 this new line formed a useful connection between the East & West Junction Railway at Stratford and the Midland Railway at Broom Junction. With the ambitious Midland Railway taking an apparent interest in East & West Junction and Northampton & Banbury Junction affairs, the local Directors were led to believe that their impecunious, under-utilised lines would achieve main line status, becoming, in the process, an important east-to-west route for Midland trains between London, Bedford, Gloucester and South Wales.

In fact, the Midland was less than enthusiastic about this new east-to-west route, and although the company would clearly have welcomed a shorter path for its goods trains between London and Gloucester, the MR Directors were reluctant to inject their own capital into schemes such as the Easton Neston Mineral & Towcester, Roade & Olney Junction Railway. The latter company was therefore forced to struggle on alone, and like the N&BJR and E&WJR back in the 1860s, the new project was unable to attract sufficient capital.

In 1882 the Easton Neston Mineral & Towcester, Roade & Olney Junction Railway (mercifully) changed its name to the Stratford-upon-Avon, Towcester & Midland Junction Railway, and reduced its share capital from £230,000 to £200,000. An Act of 1883 authorised the company to "equip, improve, and lay down rails upon the East & West Junction Railway", and empowered the two companies to be worked by a joint committee as one concern. Thereafter, the Stratford-upon-Avon, Towcester & Midland Junction spent a considerable amount of money on its own line, and on the East & West Junction, but delays caused by financial problems and the insolvency of the line's contractor prevented an early completion of the scheme.

On 13th April, 1889 the ST&MJR concluded a working agreement with the Midland Railway, and finally, on 13th April, 1891, the line from Olney to Towcester was opened for goods traffic. A passenger service was inaugurated on 1st December, and for the next few months the line was served by four up and four down trains between Olney and Towcester. Trains called intermediately at Stoke Bruern and Salcey Forest, and the service was worked by Midland tank locomotives and rolling stock.[37]

Sadly, the new services failed to attract appreciable customers, and with some trains running empty, the ST&MJR was unable to pay the Midland for working the line. The passenger service between Olney and Towcester was therefore withdrawn at the end of March 1893, but the line remained open for goods traffic — the usual practice being for East & West Junction locomotives to work through to Olney (although for a short period after April 1891 the MR had worked goods trains over the ST&MJR with its own locomotives).

The Later 19th Century

The failure of the Stratford-upon-Avon, Towcester & Midland Junction scheme ended all hopes that the Northampton & Banbury Junction or East & West Junction lines would ever rise above local status, and the N&BJR settled down to become a very rural branch, serving agricultural communities such as Slapton and Helmdon.

The line was reasonably successful in terms of traffic receipts, and although the Northampton & Banbury Junction Railway was hardly a busy route, its annual revenue compared favourably with those earned by other rural lines. In general, the line's receipts averaged around £7500 a year during the 1880s; the Directors report for the half-year ending 30th June, 1886, for example, showed a gross revenue of £3922, while earnings for the next six months (until 31st December) totalled £3913, total earnings for the whole year being £7835 for the 15 mile line — an average of £522.33 per mile per year.[38]

To put these otherwise meaningless figures into perspective it is instructive to compare the N&BJR's receipts with those recorded by other lines in the same period. The Witney Railway, for instance, earned roughly the same amount per year as the N&BJR, and its receipts for 1883, 1884 and 1885 were £8358, £8159 and £8370 respectively — admittedly on a shorter line with only two intermediate stations.[39] It is, on the other hand, unfair to compare the N&BJR to the Witney Railway because the latter railway served a manufacturing town as well as a rural community. The Derry Central Railway, in contrast, was a long, cross-country line, serving mainly agricultural villages, and as such it provides a more realistic comparison with the N&BJR. Generally speaking, the Derry Central earned about £10,000 per year on a 29¼ mile railway, and typical receipts for this County Londonderry line were £9434 in 1882, rising to £10,118 in 1883 — in other words an average of only £334 per mile per year.

The sorry case of the Derry Central enables us to view the Northampton & Banbury Junction Railway in a much more favourable light. However, the main problem facing the N&BJR was not lack of traffic, so much as an underlying burden of debt which effectively negated the line's relatively-good earning capacity. Sadly, this underlying debt could not be paid off, and in 1897 it was reported that capital expenditure up to 30th June amounted to £620,199, and the half-yearly earnings were sufficient only to pay interest on the rent charges which (at that time) were capitalised at £4070.[40]

In the meantime, the financial position of the East & West Junction Railway (and its associated companies) was no better than that of the N&BJR, and at the end of the 19th century the East & West Junction, the Stratford, Towcester & Midland Junction, and the Evesham, Redditch & Stratford-upon-Avon Junction Railway agreed that the best course of action would be to sell their undertakings to the highest bidder.

It was hoped, at one stage, that the Great Central Railway would show some benevolent interest in the East & West Junction Railway or the N&BJR, and in this context it is interesting to note that the N&BJ line played a small part during the construction of the GCR London Extension when materials were conveyed to Helmdon.

In March 1899 the E&WJ was linked to the GCR London Extension by two new spurs at Woodford, but in the event the Great Central did not display any great interest in the East & West Junction, and although the Woodford link provided the shortest route between London and Stratford-upon-Avon the GCR did not introduce through workings until 1908.

Reverting to operational matters, it would be fitting, at this point, to make some mention of the kind of motive power used on the Blisworth to Banbury line in the closing years of the 19th century. The basic N&BJR passenger service of three up and three down trains was still worked by London & North Western locomotives and rolling stock, and assuming (as seems likely) that Blisworth services were integrated with those on the Buckinghamshire line, it is reasonable to conclude that the engines used were the same as those seen on Banbury to Bletchley services. If this supposition is correct the N&BJR route would have been worked by 17 inch 'Coal Engine' 0–6–0s, 18 inch 'Fast Goods' 0–6–0s, or possibly by 2–4–2Ts of the 4 ft 6 in. or 5 ft 6 in. types.

In March 1887 the LNWR introduced a service of freight trains between Blisworth and Broom Junction, and these workings brought further North Western 0–6–0s onto the Blisworth to Towcester section of the N&BJR. At the same time, the seasonal 'Shakespeare Specials' were worked by LNWR motive power until a few East & West Junction engines were fitted with vacuum brakes, while, for a short time around 1891, Midland engines had also worked through Towcester station at the head of Olney to Broom Junction freight trains.

East & West Junction Motive Power

The East & West Junction services between Blisworth, Towcester and Stratford added further interest to the locomotive scene, and it would be useful, therefore, to make some mention of the kind of E&WJR engines seen on the eastern section of the N&BJR line.

In contrast to the Northampton & Banbury Junction, the E&WJR always worked its own train services, and for this purpose the company assembled a diverse collection of locomotives. The first engine used on the line was a Manning Wardle 0–6–0 saddle tank that had been purchased from Thomas Russell Crampton, the line's contractor. Of typical Manning Wardle design, this former contractor's locomotive dated from 1866, and became No. 1 *Kineton* in the East & West Junction locomotive list.[41]

The E&WJR hoped to work its line with a fleet of six Beyer Peacock 0–6–0s, but although the engines concerned actually worked on the line for several months, the company found that it could not afford to pay for them, and these modern locomotives were subsequently sold to the Lancashire & Yorkshire Railway. Thereafter the East & West Junction line was operated by a strange assortment of hired or borrowed engines, among them two French-built locomotives obtained from Thomas Brassey & Company.

Both of the French engines appeared on the N&BJR line. Although precise details are scarce, it seems that these European locomotives had originally been obtained by Brassey in connection with a contract in the Savoy Region. Both are likely to have been purchased from Le Chemin de Fer de Rhône et Loire in 1858; No. 4A, an outside cylinder 2–4–0 tender engine, was used on passenger services between Blisworth and Stratford until 1879, when it was transferred to the Stratford to Broom line. The engine was apparently named *Ceres*. Its companion, an 0–6–0 tender engine, worked goods traffic between Blisworth and Stratford until about 1880, when it was rebuilt as a saddle tank and sold to the Bute Trustees for use at Cardiff Docks. The engine was numbered 5A in the E&WJR list, and may have retained its original name *La Savoie* in East & West Junction service.

The use of European engines must have added an exotic element to East & West Junction operations, and this exoticism was accentuated when, in 1876, the company purchased two Fairlie engines from the Yorkshire Engine Company. The Fairlie double-bogie concept was, at that time, still something of a novelty, but the E&WJR Directors may have hoped that a powerful 0–6–6–0 would have been able to handle the heavy ore traffic that was still confidently expected to materialise. No. 1 was a classic "double-ended" 0–6–6–0, while No. 2 was a single boiler Fairlie; it is of interest to note that the 0–6–6–0 was the first engine with Walschaerts valve gear to be used in the United Kingdom.

The Fairlies were sold in 1878, and thereafter the East & West Junction line was operated with the aid of further hired or borrowed engines of various types. In 1880 the company purchased an 0–6–0 goods engine from Beyer Peacock & Co. of Manchester, and this initial purchase heralded the start of a long association with this well-known manufacturer. The new engine became No. 2 in the East & West Junction list; it had 17 in. × 24 in. cylinders and 4 ft 6 in. wheels, together with a polished brass dome and other typical Beyer Peacock features.[42]

Further engines of the same general type were delivered at intervals between 1881 and the end of the century, and by 1900 the E&WJR was operating five similar 0–6–0s, together with two standard Beyer Peacock 2–4–0Ts. There were, in addition, three former LNWR 'DX' class 0–6–0s that had been purchased in 1891/2 for use on the through MR goods trains between Olney, Towcester and Stratford. Two years earlier, in August 1888, the E&WJR had purchased a second-hand 2–4–0T from the Potteries, Shrewsbury & North Wales Railway, but this engine was later sold to the Cannock & Rugeley Collieries.

A full list of the East & West Junction locomotive fleet is given in Table 3, and while this is not a complete list of all East & West Junction engines, it will at least give some indication of the classes used on E&WJR services between Blisworth, Towcester and Stratford-upon-Avon around 1895–1900. (This list should be read in conjunction with Table 4.)

Table 3

EAST & WEST JUNCTION LOCOMOTIVES USED ON THE N&BJR LINE c.1896

E&WJR No.	wheelbase	details	disposal
1	0–6–0ST	Manning Wardle 1866	sold 1910
1	2–4–0T	Yorkshire Engine Co.	sold for colliery use 1895
2	0–6–0	Beyer Peacock 1880	to LMS 1923 (*Table 4*)
3	0–6–0	Beyer Peacock 1881	to LMS 1923 (*Table 4*)
4	0–6–0	Beyer Peacock 1885	to LMS 1923 (*Table 4*)
5	2–4–0T	Beyer Peacock 1885	sold to WD 1916
6	2–4–0T	Beyer Peacock 1885	sold to WD 1916
7	0–6–0	LNWR 1863	withdrawn 1920
8	0–6–0	LNWR 1863	sold c.1910
9	0–6–0	LNWR 1866	sold 1903
10	0–6–0	Beyer Peacock 1895	to LMS 1923 (*Table 4*)
11	0–6–0	Beyer Peacock 1896	to LMS 1923 (*Table 4*)
12	0–6–0	Beyer Peacock 1900	to LMS 1923 (*Table 4*)

Passenger rolling stock used on N&BJR and East & West Junction services were all 4- or 6-wheelers, the coaches used between Blisworth and Banbury being LNWR stock, while their counterparts on the E&WJR line were all owned by the East & West Junction company.

Sources for Chapter Three

30. *Bradshaw's Shareholders Manual,* 1864.
31. Northampton & Banbury Junction Railway minutes.
32. Northampton & Banbury Junction Railway, Half-Year Reports.
33. *Ibid.*
34. C.R.H. Simpson, The Northampton & Banbury Junction Railway, *The Locomotive.*
35. *The Railway Times,* August 1875.
36. *Bradshaw's Shareholders Manuals.*
37. *The Locomotive Magazine.*
38. Northampton & Banbury Junction Railway, Half-Year Reports.
39. Witney Railway Half-Year Reports.
40. Northampton & Banbury Junction Railway, Half-Year Reports.
41. *The Railway Magazine,* April 1910; *The Locomotive Magazine.*
42. *The Locomotive Magazine.*

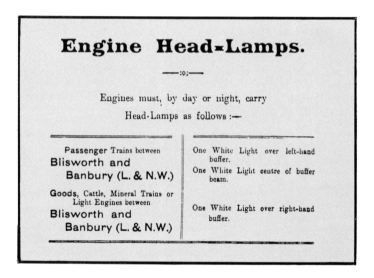

Extract from the Working Appendix giving details of engine headlamp codes for the line.

Chapter Four
The Twentieth Century (1900–1948)

The Edwardian period was, without doubt, the golden age of Britain's railways. In those halycon years great companies such as the Midland and the London & North Western held an undisputed monopoly of land transport. Railways were at the "leading edge" of Britain's world-beating industrial technology, and at a time when rural communities such as Helmdon and Wappenham still moved at the speed of a horse, the familiar steam railways — which now reached into every corner of the land — were the fastest, safest and most efficient means of transport on earth.

Most railway companies managed to pay some form of dividend, and although such prosperity did not extend to the debt-laden Northampton & Banbury Junction Railway, the company usually managed to show a small surplus of income over expenditure. Traffic receipts were, moreover, on the increase, and by the turn-of-the-century, the railway's annual takings had reached £8000. Receipts for the six months ending 31st December, 1901 totalled £4229, a small increase over the corresponding half-year ending 31st December, 1900; expenditure, for the period June–December 1901, totalled £4169, and these figures enabled the company to declare a nominal "profit" of £60.[43]

Edwardian train services were little different to those offered to the public during the 19th century. The October 1911 timetable, for instance, was similar to its 1888 predecessor, and local travellers were still given a choice of just three up and three down passenger trains. The first up train left Banbury at 7.25 am and arrived in Blisworth at 8.20. A balancing down working ran from Blisworth to Banbury at 9.13 am, and the timetable suggests that this same train turned round at Banbury to form the 10.40 am up service. The third up service of the day left Banbury at 6.02 pm, and reached Blisworth by 7.00; finally, at 7.30 pm a balancing down service left Blisworth. A special market train ran from Blisworth to Banbury at 2.10 pm on Thursdays-only, and there was a corresponding return working from Banbury at 3.35 pm (Thursdays-only). Additionally, there were several short distance workings between Blisworth and Towcester (including the above mentioned 2.10 pm, which terminated at Towcester on non-market days). The Blisworth to Towcester line was also served by two up and two down Stratford-upon-Avon trains, together with a solitary early morning service from Blisworth to Woodford. No Sunday services were provided and regular Sunday trains were never a feature of N&BJR operation.

The Stratford-upon-Avon & Midland Junction Railway

As we have seen, the East & West Junction Railway and its associates (the Evesham, Redditch & Stratford-upon-Avon Junction Railway and the Stratford, Towcester & Midland Junction Railway) had agreed, at the end of the 19th century, that the only answer to their financial problems would be a sale to one or other of the main line companies, and to facilitate this aim the three local companies obtained a further Act of Parliament. The Midland Counties Junction Railways (Sales) Act, which received the Royal Assent on 17th August, 1901, empowered the Joint Committee running the E&WJR,

Three of the Beyer Peacock 0−6−0 locomotives that belonged to the Stratford and Midland Junction Railway and ran on the Banbury Branch.

A standard composite coach of the SMJ Railway that was used on the Banbury branch.

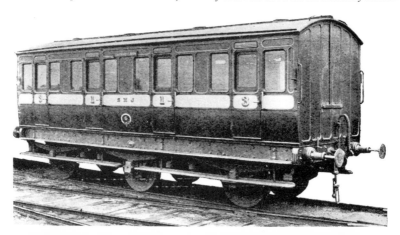

ER&SJR and ST&MJR system to sell their entire undertaking to the Midland, Great Western, Great Central or London & North Western companies. Unfortunately, none of these large companies wished to purchase the unremunerative local lines, and the East & West Junction Railway and its threadbare partners retained their unwanted independence.

Unable to divest themselves of the three railways, the proprietors decided that a complete restructuring of their system was necessary, and on 1st August, 1908 the local companies were formally amalgamated into a single company, with capital powers of £600,000 and borrowing powers of £200,000. Although the new company was, in effect, merely an enlarged East & West Junction Railway, the Directors decided to rename their undertaking The Stratford-upon-Avon & Midland Junction Railway.

In August 1908 Russell Willmott (1879–1920) was appointed S&MJR General Manager, and under his energetic leadership the new organisation was able to initiate several small, but encouraging improvements. One of the most important of these changes concerned the line's poorly-maintained trackwork, which was thoroughly overhauled under the new management. The resulting improvements were noted by local travellers, and also by The Railway Magazine, which in April 1910 stated that:

> Travelling is much easier than it used to be, thanks to the care and attention now given to the permanent way, which has been thoroughly overhauled and strengthened. The growth of grass and weeds that gave the track of the old East and West Junction Railway a somewhat derelict appearance, has been uprooted, and no more vegetation is apparent on the road-bed of the Stratford-upon-Avon and Midland Junction Railway than on any other well-kept line. The fences and level crossing gates have been substantially-repaired and now effectively fulfil the purposes for which they were provided. By a careful rearrangement of the duties of the permanent way men, these improvements had been attained without additional expense, although the wages of the staff have been increased in many cases. Attention has been given to bridges, and, where necessary, the under-structures have been strengthened in substantial manner.[44]

The Stratford-upon-Avon & Midland Junction Railway did not, as yet, control the Northampton & Banbury Junction Railway, which maintained a stubborn and somewhat aloof independence. This was, at least in part, an inevitable concomitant of the line's entirely separate history and traditions, but there were, nevertheless, compelling reasons for the N&BJR to be brought into the S&MJR fold — after all, the Blisworth to Greens Norton section of the Northampton & Banbury Junction line formed an integral part of the Stratford-upon-Avon & Midland Junction "main line".

It was necessary, before the desired amalgamation could take place, for another approach to be made to Parliament, and in 1910 a fresh Bill was deposited. This new Bill received the Royal Assent on 29th April, 1910, and the Stratford-upon-Avon & Midland Junction Railway was thereby empowered to purchase the Northampton & Banbury Junction line between Blisworth and Cockley Brake Junction. The 1910 Act contained provisions relating to running powers over the LNWR between Cockley Brake Junction and Banbury Merton Street, and also allowed the S&MJR to operate motor buses and open refreshment rooms.

[10 Edw. 7.]   *Stratford-upon-Avon and Midland*   [**Ch. viii.**]
Junction Railway (Various Powers) Act, 1910.

CHAPTER viii.

An Act for transferring to and vesting in the Stratford-
upon-Avon and Midland Junction Railway Company the
undertaking of the Northampton and Banbury Junction
Railway Company to confer further powers on the
Stratford-upon-Avon and Midland Junction Railway
Company and for other purposes.   [29th April 1910.]

A.D. 1910.

WHEREAS the Stratford-upon-Avon and Midland Junction
Railway Company (in this Act called "the Company")
were incorporated by the Stratford-upon-Avon and Midland
Junction Railway (Amalgamation) Act 1908 by an amalgamation
of the East and West Junction Railway Company the Evesham
Redditch and Stratford - upon - Avon Junction Railway Company
and the Stratford-upon-Avon Towcester and Midland Junction
Railway Company for the purpose of carrying on as one undertaking the undertakings of such companies:

And wlereas by the Northampton and Banbury Junction
Railway Act 1863 the Northampton and Banbury Junction Railway
Company (in this Act called "the Northampton Company") were
incorporated and by that Act the Northampton and Banbury
Railway (Branch) Act 1865 the Northampton and Banbury
Railway (Extensions) Act 1865 the Northampton and Banbury
Junction Railway Act 1866 and the Northampton and Banbury
Junction Railway Act 1870 the Northampton Company were
authorised to construct the railways and works as in those Acts
described in the county of Northampton and certain portions
of such railways and works have been constructed by the
Northampton Company:

[*Price* 2s. 3d.]

The act transferring the powers of the N&BJR to the SMJ Railway.

As a result of the amalgamation, Blisworth to Banbury train services were worked by S&MJR locomotives and rolling stock instead of the LNWR engines and coaches that had hitherto been employed. As mentioned in Chapter Three, Beyer Peacock 0–6–0s found much favour on the S&MJR, and it is likely that these sturdy, workmanlike machines would have worked both passenger and goods traffic between Blisworth and Banbury. Ordinary travellers are unlikely to have taken much notice of the changed motive power situation, although those with a deeper interest in railways may have reflected that the use of Beyer Peacock locomotives over single lines had much in common with Irish practice (the Belfast & County Down Railway, for example, was a predominantly single track system of comparable size to the S&MJR; it was, for most of its life, worked exclusively by Beyer Peacock engines).

Another concomitant of the 1910 amalgamation concerned the status of the Greens Norton to Cockley Brake line which became, under S&MJ auspices, a less important route than the main Blisworth to Stratford-upon-Avon line. As if to underline this changed situation, the S&MJ authorities removed some recently-laid N&BJR chaired trackwork and relaid it on the "main line", while at the same time former East & West Junction permanent way material was used on the Cockley Brake line.

In purely visual terms the amalgamation was accompanied by one or two small livery changes, and having experimented, for a time, with blue engines and reddish-brown carriages the S&MJ later standardised on a simple, lined black locomotive livery. Passenger vehicles, meanwhile, received cream upper panels, although some coaches sported a wide cream band between reddish-brown upper and lower panels. (The basic body colour was described as "lake", but it must have been more brown than red because, in 1910, *The Railway Magazine* spoke of *chocolate* and cream coaches on the S&MJR system.)

In August 1914, a period of growing international tension in the Balkans (and elsewhere) culminated in an unprovoked German attack on France and Belgium, and in an inevitable response to this international outrage, the British government declared war on the Teutonic aggressors. The United Kingdom thereby became involved in a major European conflict for the first time in over a hundred years, and the previously settled period was brought to a sudden and brutal close.

As far as Britain's railways were concerned, the 1914–18 war resulted in a vast increase of emergency traffic, and many routes became of vital strategic importance as men and munitions were rushed to the Channel ports prior to embarkation for the Western Front. The situation was rather different on rural lines such as the Northampton & Banbury Junction line, and whereas neighbouring main lines such as the GWR and LNWR carried extra traffic, the N&BJR suffered a reduction in its already meagre services. In September 1915, for example, the pre-war train service of three up and three down workings remained in force, with departures from Banbury at 7.15, 10.35 am, and 6.02 pm, and corresponding return services from Blisworth at 9.20 am, 4.50 and 7.38 pm respectively; an afternoon market train ran through from Blisworth to Banbury at 2.20 pm on Thursdays Only, the return working from Banbury to Blisworth being at 3.35 pm (ThO). Within a few months, however, the exigencies of total war had taken their toll, and the Blisworth to Banbury line was left with a minimal service of just two trains each way.

The August 1917 timetable is typical of that in force in the later stages of World War I, with a morning departure from Blisworth at 9.25 am and an afternoon working at 6.00 pm. In the reverse direction, up services left Banbury at 10.45 am and 4.30 pm, reaching Blisworth by 11.40 am and 5.25 pm respectively.

This depleted train service persisted, with only minor modifications, until the line was finally closed in 1951; in July 1922, for instance, the morning down train left Blisworth at 9.18 am and returned from Banbury at 10.30 am, while additional up and down trains left Blisworth at 5.23 pm and Banbury at 4.55 pm. A peculiarity of the 1922 timetable concerned the provision of a solitary 7.30 am up working from Helmdon to Towcester on Wednesdays and Saturdays only. Goods services consisted of an afternoon through working which reached Banbury at 4.10 pm and departed for Blisworth at 6.55 pm. This freight working called at Farthinghoe in the down direction, but not in the up, because the single goods siding at that station could not easily be shunted by eastbound trains. (Additional goods and passenger trains served the Blisworth to Towcester section which, as we have seen, formed part of the S&MJ main line to Stratford-upon-Avon.)

Demand for iron ore during World War I did much to stimulate mining in the Oxfordshire/Northamptonshire region, and in 1920 an industrial line, known as the Edge Hill Light Railway, was opened from Burton Bassett, on the S&MR to an ironstone quarry on Edge Hill. The new line was worked by two ex-London Brighton & South Coast Railway "Terrier" 0−6−0Ts, numbered 1 and 2, and purchased in 1919 and 1920 respectively; the engines concerned were former LB&SCR Nos. 73 and 74 *Deptford* and *Shadwell*.

Sadly, the Edge Hill Light Railway failed to prosper, though in the short term its opening seemed to guarantee much-needed traffic for the S&MJ. It seemed at the time that the line from Blisworth to Stratford (and even its branch to Banbury) was on the threshold of prosperity, and this optimistic view was certainly shared by *The Railway Magazine* which, in September 1919 printed a favourable report on the line:

Originally designed to develop the large iron ore traffic and furnish a shorter route for it from Northamptonshire into South Wales, the Stratford-upon-Avon & Midland Junction Railway today serves many other useful purposes. It forms a connecting link for goods traffic between the main lines of the Midland, Great Central, and London & North Western Railways, and is within easy reach of the Warwickshire and Midland coalfields. There are immense quantities of ironstone in the district in addition to large quantities of limestone. These facts, coupled with the circumstance that there is much cheap land adjacent to the railway suitable for blast furnaces, factories and works, indicate that in the near future there is likely to be considerable industrial development in the districts served by the Stratford-upon-Avon & Midland Junction line, particularly in Northamptonshire, and in that part of Warwickshire adjoining the former county. Under the capable management that controls it, the railway ought to secure a considerable share of the advantages that should accrue from the promotion of the various schemes for the reconstruction of industry that are now occupying the minds of businessmen.[45]

The Grouping and After

In the meantime the government had decided that as an alternative to outright nationalisation, the diverse railway companies that constituted much of the transport system of Great Britain would be "grouped" into four large regional companies, and on 1st January, 1923 the "Big Four" railways were created under the terms of the Transport Act 1921. As a result of this great amalgamation, the number of British Railway companies was reduced from 58 to 20 (i.e. the big four companies plus sixteen smaller undertakings).

The Stratford-upon-Avon & Midland Junction Railway became part of the newly-created London Midland & Scottish Railway, although it is interesting to note that the S&MJ was not formally dissolved until March 1923. In the short term, this change of ownership resulted in very few changes, and most ordinary travellers would have been blissfully unaware that an organisational upheaval had taken place. Railway enthusiasts, on the other hand, feared that the S&MJ's non-standard locomotive fleet would not fare well under the new administration, and sure enough, five former S&MJ engines were withdrawn in the first year of LMS ownership, the locomotives concerned being Nos. 3, 7, 10, 13 and 15.

Ironically, this list of casualties included the S&MJ's latest engine — a former London Brighton & South Coast Railway "Jumbo" class heavy goods 0–6–0 that had been purchased second-hand from the LB&SCR in 1920. Dating from 1884, this south coast veteran became S&MJ No. 7, having replaced one of the former LNWR 0–6–0s in the S&MJ list.

These initial withdrawals left eight former Stratford-upon-Avon & Midland Junction locomotives in commission, and by 1925 the survivors included Nos. 2, 4, 11, 12, 14, 16, 17 and 18. All of the engines taken over in 1923 were re-numbered by the LMS as shown in the following table.

Table 4

		S&MJ LOCOMOTIVES TAKEN OVER BY THE LMS IN 1923			
SMJ No.	LMS No.	wheelbase	details		withdrawn
2	2300	0–6–0	Beyer Peacock	1880	1926
3	2301	0–6–0	Beyer Peacock	1881	1924
4	2302	0–6–0	Beyer Peacock	1885	1929
7	2303	0–6–0	Brighton Works	1884	1924
10	2304	0–6–0	Beyer Peacock	1895	1924
11	2305	0–6–0	Beyer Peacock	1896	1930
12	2306	0–6–0	Beyer Peacock	1900	1930
13	290	2–4–0	Beyer Peacock	1903	1924
14	2307	0–6–0	Beyer Peacock	1903	1926
15	2308	0–6–0	Beyer Peacock	1904	1924
16	2309	0–6–0	Beyer Peacock	1906	1927
17	2310	0–6–0	Beyer Peacock	1908	1925
18	2311	0–6–0	Beyer Peacock	1908	1927

In October 1923 *The Railway Magazine* reported that passenger locomotives belonging to the London Midland & Scottish Railway were being
painted "in the style formerly standardised by the Midland Railway, namely
a dark red, with black-panelling and yellow lines", but it is unclear if this
style of painting was applied to any of the former S&MJ engines, which
presumably went to the scrap yards in black livery. In any case, the last
S&MJ engines (Nos. 2305 and 2306) were withdrawn in August 1930, and
thereafter LMS locomotives — especially standard MR 0–6–0s — reigned
supreme on the former East & West Junction and Northampton & Banbury
Junction lines.

Although the elimination of non-standard locomotives was inevitably
seen by enthusiasts as a somewhat negative result of the LMS takeover, the
new company realised that the lines from Blisworth and Ravenstone Wood
Junction to Stratford were valuable diversionary routes for cross-country
goods traffic, and the S&MJ line was extensively rebuilt during the 1920s to
bring it up to main line standards. Trackwork, for example, was renewed in
1927–28, while at the same time the LMS equipped the route with signalling
apparatus for "long section" working.

Having invested much-needed new capital into the route, the company
diverted a considerable number of Bristol to London goods trains over the
line between Broom Junction, Towcester and Ravenstone Wood, and in the
next few years the S&MJ became a relatively important freight artery carrying fast perishable traffic between Avonmouth and London.

Train Services in the LMS Era

The LMS authorities were well aware that Stratford-upon-Avon had
become a major tourist attraction, and in an attempt to exploit this source of
leisure traffic to its fullest potential (and perhaps snatch traffic from the rival
GWR) the company opened the 'Welcome Hotel' at Stratford and introduced
new train services on the line from Blisworth. In an innovative move, the
LMS operating authorities provided a fast, limited-stop evening train from
Stratford-upon-Avon to Blisworth — at which point good connections were
available to London Euston. This new train, which left Stratford at 4.30 pm
and reached Blisworth by 5.32 pm, was introduced in 1931. In the return
direction, a balancing down working left Blisworth at 6.00 pm, and arrived
back in Stratford at 7.10. The train called *en route* at Towcester, but otherwise ran non-stop in both directions.

A few months later, in April 1932 an attempt was made to provide door-
to-door service for patrons of the Welcome Hotel when the LMS introduced
a novel vehicle known as "The Ro-Railer" between Blisworth and Stratford.
Built by Karrier Motors Ltd of Huddersfield, the Ro-Railer was designed by J.
Shearman, the LMSR's road motor engineer. Externally, this unusual vehicle
looked like an ordinary road vehicle that had been adapted for rail operation, although, as *The Railway Magazine* noticed in March 1931, its buffers
and draw gear gave it "an individual note", while observant travellers would
have noted "the flanged wheels mounted on the axles on the inner sides of
the pneumatic-tyred road wheels". The bus-type body could accommodate
26 passengers, and had been constructed by Cravens Ltd of Sheffield;

BROOM JUNCTION, STRATFORD-ON-AVON, BANBURY
and BLISWORTH (ONE CLASS ONLY.)

WEEK DAYS.

Gloucester ....dep.						8 50		1|37					4|28		6|51
Cheltenham Spa (Lansdown) ,,						9 5		1 53					4	45		7 8
Tewkesbury .... ,,						9 0		1|39					4|50		7 8
Ashchurch .... ,,				7 10		9 25		2 9					5 8		7 27
Evesham .... ,,				7 42		10 44		2|39					5|43		8 1
Broom Junction ....arr.				7 50		11 2		2|55					6 0		8|24
Birmingham (New St.).....dep.			6 32			9 51		1|B10					5 0		7|30
Redditch .... ,,			7 27			10 37		2|13					5|55		8 17
Alcester .... ,,			7 44			10 55		2|32					6 15		8|38
Broom Junction ....arr.			7 52			11 3		2|40					6|23		8 46
Broom Junction ....dep.			8 20			11 15		3 5					6 30		8	55
Bidford-on-Avon .... ,,			8 25			11 20		3 9					6|35		8|59
Binton .... ,,			8 33			11 25		3 17					6|43		9|S07
Stratford-on-Avon { arr.		7 45	8 41			11 35		3 25					6	50		9 15
{ dep.	7 45				12	15		4	30				6 15		9	S017
Ettington .... ,,	8 0				12	27		4	42				6	27		9	S029
Kineton .... ,,	8 14				12	37		4	49				6	35		9	S036
Fenny Compton .... ,,	8 30				12	49						6	47		
Byfield ....arr.	8 45				1 2						6	59		
Byfield ....dep.	8 52	9 55			1	15		2	20				7	13		9	58
Woodford & Hinton............ ,,	8 57	9 59			1	20		2	25				7	18		10 3
London (Marylebone) ....arr.	10 48	11	10			2	55		4	57				9 0		
Woodford & Hinton............dep.	8 37				1 0		3	35		2	SX 7				
Byfield .... ,,	8 42				1 5		3	40		2	SX12				
Byfield ....dep.	8 57				1 7		3	45		4	SX46		7 4		
Morton Pinkney (for Sulgrave)...	9 7				1	17		3	55		4	SX56		7	14		
Blakesley .... ,,	9 20				1	24		4 2		5	3		7	21		
Towcester ....arr.	9 28				1	32		4	10		5	11		7	29		
Banbury (Merton Street)...dep.			10 40							5 5				
Farthinghoe .... ,,			10 49							5	14				
Helmdon .... ,,			11 2							5	27				
Wappenham .... ,,			11 11							5	36				
Towcester ....arr.			11 18							5	45				
Towcester ....dep.	8 2	9 32		11 21	12|50		1|35		4|11		5|12	5|46	7|33
Blisworth .... ,,	8 12	9 41		11 30	1 0		1	48		4	20		5	21	5	59	7	42
Northampton (Castle) ......arr.	8 32	9 57		11 58	7|29		2| 5		4|47		5|52	6|38	8|12
Rugby .... ,,	9 16	10|1		1J 2	2|10|0		2|26		5| 4			7|047	8|047
Bedford (St. John's) .... ,,	10A 8	12	11			2K34		3 53					7	45	10	41
London (Euston) .... ,,	9Q53	11|25		12|42	2|41		4| 0				7| 0	8|40	10Q23

WEEK DAYS.

London (Euston) ....dep.	....	7 0			9Y30	12| 5			2| 7		30 6		4|35	4|35	70 0	70 0	9S45
Bedford (St. John's) .... ,,		6 30			9Q44	12 16			2|50		3| 8			6| 0	6|50	70 0	8|20
Rugby .... ,,		8D 3	8 35	12|52	1|50			7D13		3D18		5|45	5|45	8|15	8|15	9 4.
Northampton (Castle) ...... ,,		8 40	9 0	12|55	2 9			4|20		5|16		6|12	6|12	8|25	9| 3	10|20
Blisworth ....dep.	....	8 55		9 20	1|25	2|32			4|36		5 35		6|27	6|30	8 50	9|19	11| 6.
Towcester ....arr.		9 4		9 29	1|34	2|41			4|45		5|44		6|36	6|39	8|59	9|28	11 16
Towcester ....dep.				9 31							5|46						
Wappenham .... ,,				9 40							5|55						
Helmdon .... ,,				9 49							6| 4						
Farthinghoe .... ,,				10 1							6|17						
Banbury (Merton Street)...arr.	....			10 9							6|25						
Towcester ....dep.	....	9 7		Stop	1|36	2|42			4|15	4|46			6|37	6|40	Stop	9|29	11|15
Blakesley .... ,,		9 16			1 44	2|50			4|23	4|53			6|45	6|48		9|37	11|22
Morton Pinkney (for Sulgrave)...		9 26			1|51	2|57			4|30				6|52	6|55		9|44	
Byfield ....arr.		9 36			2| 0	3| 5			4|39				7| 0	7| 3		9|53	Stop
Byfield ....dep.		9 55			2|20			3|15					7|13	7|13		9|58	
Woodford & Hinton............arr.		9 59			2|25			3|20					7|18	7|18		70, 3	
London (Marylebone) ....dep.	..	6 40	10 0		12|15								6|20	7|30	
Woodford & Hinton............dep.	8 37	9 28	1 0		2 7								7|47	10|11	
Byfield ....arr.	8 42	9 28	1 5		2|12								7|52	10|16	
Byfield ....dep.	Stop	9 38			2|17								7|54		
Fenny Compton .... ,,		9 51			2|31								8| 6		
Kineton .... ,,	10 4			2	43			5	0				8 17		9	46
Ettington .... ,,	10 13			2	53			5	9				8	26		9	54
Stratford-on-Avon { arr.		10 24		3 4			5	19				8 37		10	4
{ dep.	7 22	10 28	2	15			5	26		7	40				
Binton .... ,,	7 31	10 36	2	24			5	39		7S04				
Bidford-on-Avon .... ,,	7 40	10 44	2	33			5	47		7	57				
Broom Junction ....arr.	7 43	10 47	2	36			5	50		8 0				
Broom Junction ....dep.	8 1	11 5	2	56			6	1		8	27				
Alcester ....arr.	8 11	11 15	3 3			6	11		8	34				
Redditch .... ,,	8 30	11 34	3 22			6	32		8	51				
Birmingham (New St.)......... ,,	9 5	12	25	4 7			7	47		9 36				
Broom Junction ....dep.	8 0	9 54	11 5	2	55			6	24		8	47				
Evesham ....arr.	8 19	10	9 11	20	3	12			6	39		9	2			
Ashchurch .... ,,	9 15	10 43	11 45	3	51			7	14		9 34				
Tewkesbury .... ,,	9 25	11	0 12	7	4 40			7	36					
Cheltenham Spa (Lansdown) ,,	..	11	1 11 58	4	34			7	36		11 0				
Gloucester .... ,,		11 15	12	12	4	59			7	48		11 16				

LMS Country Lorry Services

Link manufacturers and distributors with customers in rural Districts.

Ask the LMS Agent for particulars.

A Via Northampton on Saturdays.
B 1.18 p.m. on Saturdays.
B Via Northampton.
J Saturdays only. Via Northampton. Arrives 12.46 p.m. on December 23rd and 24th, 1936, and March 25th, 1937.
K On Saturdays arrives 3.38 p.m.

L Via Northampton; arrives 12.0noon on Saturdays.
Q On Saturdays arrives 10.15 a.m. via Northampton.
SO Saturdays only.
SX Saturdays excepted.
Y Via Northampton; leaves 10.40 a.m. on Saturdays.

The LMS passenger timetable for September 1936.

another firm involved in the project was the Lang Wheel Company, which had provided the steel rail wheels.[46]

The Ro-Railer ran from Blisworth station, through Towcester, to Stratford goods yard, at which point it left the railway and, making use of its rubber tyred road wheels, proceeded through the town to its destination. Sadly, the Ro-Railer service was withdrawn in June 1932, after a trial period of operation lasting only two months. Mechanical problems had contributed to the vehicle's early demise, but the main reason for its untimely withdrawal was lack of passengers. Although the 101 mile journey from Euston to Stratford-upon-Avon compared favourably with the 102¾ mile Great Western route from Paddington, most travellers preferred the long-established GWR services, and the S&MJR line never lived up to its claim to be "The Shakespeare Route".

On a footnote, it is worth recalling that the LNER continued to offer a daily through carriage in each direction between Marylebone, Woodford and Stratford — although this service did not use any part of the former Northampton & Banbury Junction section. In the early 1930s, the through service left Stratford SMJ station at 7.45 am and reached Marylebone at 10.48, while in the reverse direction travellers on the 6.20 pm from Marylebone were able to reach Stratford by 8.37, their coach having been slipped at Woodford. Sadly, this service was itself withdrawn on 1st February, 1936.[47]

The Ro-Railer and other LMS-initiated developments were concerned primarily with the SMJ "main line", and there was little attempt to stimulate traffic on what had now become a "branch" service between Towcester and Banbury. Indeed, the 1930s train service was worse than that provided during the Edwardian period, and intending travellers on the former N&BJR were offered a choice of just two up and two down workings to and from Banbury.

The August 1935 timetable is typical of the LMS period, with two trains in each direction between Blisworth and Banbury. Daily operation began with the departure of the 9.20 am morning service from Blisworth, and this first up working arrived in Banbury at 10.09. At 10.40 am, the train returned to Blisworth, calling at all stations en route and arriving at 11.30. There was, thereafter, an enormous gap in the passenger timetable, and travellers from Banbury to Blisworth were faced with a long and boring wait until the second up train of the day departed from Banbury at 5.05 pm. Meanwhile, another train had left Blisworth at 5.35 pm, and this down working passed the 5.05 pm ex-Banbury at Towcester before arriving in Banbury at 6.25; continuing its journey in the opposite direction at 5.46 pm, the up train reached Blisworth at 5.59.

The Blisworth to Towcester section was served by 3 up and 4 down trains which continued through over the SMJ "main line" to Stratford-upon-Avon, and there were in addition a handful of short-distance workings between Blisworth and Towcester, or Towcester and Byfield. These extra workings ensured that the people of Towcester enjoyed a comparatively good train service of about 8 trains each way to and from Blisworth.

Goods Traffic

Goods services were confined to one through freight train each way, although, as in the case of passenger trains, there was additional traffic via Towcester (including two regular through freight workings between Olney and Broom Junction). Cattle trains were occasionally run on an "as required" basis, especially on Thursdays, when Banbury cattle market attracted dealers from far and wide.

Coal inwards and agricultural traffic outwards continued to form the main types of originating freight traffic, and goods vehicles seen on the line reflected this limited range of commodities. Generally speaking, 5- or 7-plank opens predominated, together with covered vans used to convey perishables or general merchandise.

The intermediate stations were equipped with loading docks and cattle pens, but covered goods sheds were found only at Towcester and Helmdon. Successive editions of The Railway Clearing House *Handbook of Stations* are a useful source of information about the kind of goods accommodation provided at each station, and the following table (based upon the 1938 edition) shows the facilities available at each place.

Table 5

GOODS AND PASSENGER ACCOMMODATION ON THE BLISWORTH TO
BANBURY LINE

station	distance	accommodation						crane power	
Blisworth SMJ	00m 00ch	G	P		L	H		-	
Towcester	04m 15ch	G	P	F	L	H	C	1 ton	10 cwt
Wappenham	08m 07ch	G	P		L	H		-	
Helmdon	11m 59ch	G	P	F	L	H	C	1 ton	10 cwt
Farthinghoe	16m 50ch	G	P		L	H		-	
Banbury LMS	20m 53ch	G	P	F	L	H	C	5 tons	0 cwt

G = goods; P = passengers; F = furniture vans, portable engines, etc.; L = livestock;
H = horse boxes & prize cattle vans; C = carriages & motor cars.

It will be seen that each station could handle goods and passenger traffic but facilities for certain specialised forms of goods traffic were found only at Towcester, Helmdon and Banbury. All of the stations had cattle docks (indicated by 'L' in the table) but the absence of 'F' and 'C' reveals that Wappenham, Blisworth SMJ and Farthinghoe did not have end-loading docks with convenient access for vehicular traffic or bulky items such as furniture or machinery. Fixed cranes were available at Towcester, Helmdon and Banbury, but travelling cranes could be sent to the smaller stations if required.

The 1938 *Handbook* does not show any private sidings on the Northampton & Banbury Junction section, although there had, at one time, been an ironstone siding between Blisworth and Towcester.

BROOM JUNCTION, STRATFORD-ON-AVON, BANBURY, and BLISWORTH—(One class only).

Bradshaw's passenger timetable for July 1938.

Table 266   BROOM JUNCTION, STRATFORD-ON-AVON, BANBURY, and BLISWORTH (Third class only)

LMS wartime passenger service for July 1942.

LMS class '4F', 0−6−0 No. 4343 leaves Banbury on 11th September, 1939; the engine was one of the LMS built '4Fs'.   *H.C. Casserley*

Class '4F' 0−6−0 No. 43773 waits at Banbury Merton Street with the 4.45 pm afternoon service to Blisworth on 29th June, 1951; engines usually ran tender-first between Banbury and Blisworth in the years following World War II.   *John Edgington*

Locomotives in the LMS Era

The relatively long distances between Blisworth and Banbury, or Blisworth and Stratford-upon-Avon, dictated that tender locomotives were the most suitable types for use on the N&BJR and S&MJR lines. As we have seen, 0–6–0 goods engines found much favour on the SMJ, and such engines continued to be used on the route throughout the LMS and BR eras. The SMJ lines were placed in the Midland Division after 1923, and, not surprisingly, former Midland 0–6–0s soon began to appear in increasing numbers. Typical locos, around 1930, included small-boiler Johnson 0–6–0s Nos. 3695 and 3696, together with standard class '3F' 0–6–0s Nos. 3521, 3529 and 3698. The older, Johnson class '2F' engines were perhaps more characteristic during the early 1930s, but '3Fs' eventually became the most usual type. Another type seen on the line around 1930 were former Lancashire & Yorkshire 0–6–0s, but it is said that local enginemen disliked these "foreigners", and much preferred the ubiquitous Midland engines.

Locomotives were usually turned at the end of each trip, and for this purpose small turntables were provided at Blisworth, Banbury and Towcester. All three were of 41–42 ft diameter, providing sufficient room for the 0–6–0 tender engines used on Northampton & Banbury Junction services.

Although '2F' or '3F' 0–6–0s remained the usual form of motive power during the 1930s, the more powerful '4F' variants appeared towards the end of the LMS era, and were probably in regular use during World War II.

World War II

The outbreak of war on Sunday 3rd September, 1939 did not produce any immediate changes on the Blisworth to Banbury line, and despite early fears of a massive aerial attack, the first months of the conflict were so quiet that people spoke derisively of a "Phoney War". The fall of France in June 1940 dispelled any illusions about the gravity of the situation, and in fear of imminent invasion, the government ordered that all road signs and station nameboards should be taken down. Blackout regulations were rigorously enforced, and in a further attempt to confuse enemy pilots, a huge dummy "railway yard" was constructed in a remote position to the west of Banbury; in the event of an attack it was proposed that this dummy yard would be set alight — thereby attracting further raiders who might otherwise have placed their bombs on the real junction facilities.

The threat of massive air raids was, in fact, taken very seriously, and basing their estimations upon known casualty figures available from World War I, government "experts" predicted that the *Luftwaffe* would drop about 950 tons of bombs per day, resulting in 2 million casualties within the first six months. Whole cities were expected to be knocked out, and faced with this dreadful scenario (which was so appalling that it was withheld from public scrutiny) the government identified a variety of alternative supply routes between industrial centres and the Channel ports. One of these routes was the S&MJ line which, being remote from major cities, was thought to be relatively safe from bombing; the line was, as a result, improved in various ways, and for a time the route from Broom Junction via Stratford and Towcester carried additional wartime traffic.

Happily, pre-war estimates of likely wartime damage were wildly inaccurate, and although Banbury was bombed by a lone raider in 1940, World War II was less destructive than had been feared. Ironically, German cities suffered much greater damage than their British counterparts, and in order to mount a gigantic air offensive against Europe, the Royal Air Force embarked on an unprecedented expansion programme. Aerodromes appeared all over southern England, and with petrol rationing in force, these new air fields were often supplied from nearby railway stations. Northamptonshire had its fair share of RAF stations, and by June 1944 there were at least three such aerodromes within the Towcester area. All of these were conveniently close to the N&BJR or other lines. RAF Silverstone, for instance, could be reached from either Towcester or Wappenham stations, while RAF Hinton-in-the-Hedges could be supplied from Farthinghoe, from Brackley (LMS) or from Brackley (LNER). Another airfield was located at Turweston, to the east of Brackley (but accessible also from Wappenham or Towcester). These aerodromes were used for differing purposes throughout the war, but by June 1944 RAF Silverstone was a Coastal Command Operational Training Unit operating Wellingtons and Hurricanes, while Hinton-in-the-Hedges was used by a "Signals Development Unit"; RAF Turweston was a satellite station for nearby Silverstone.

Wartime passenger services were merely a continuation of those provided in the 1930s, with departures from Banbury to Blisworth at 10.40 am and 5.00 pm, and return workings from Blisworth at 9.20 am and 5.30 pm. This meagre pattern of services still required two locomotives and train sets, and it was usual for the up and down afternoon trains to pass each other in Towcester station at 5.40 pm.

In physical terms the war produced few changes on the Blisworth to Banbury line, and apart from the large numbers of people in uniform, there was little obvious sign that there was "a war on". The empty nameboards were, nevertheless, visible reminders that tiny stations such as Helmdon and Wappenham were involved — however remotely — in a major conflict, and at a time when the mysterious "fifth columnists" were considered to be a very real threat, most travellers welcomed the removal of station nameboards on the basis that *something* was being done to combat the Nazi threat!

The omnipresent blackout was another obvious reminder of the war, and despite the fact that wartime train services on the N&BJR line did not entail much after-dark passenger business (at least not at Wappenham or Helmdon) platform lamps were painted-out, leaving a narrow gap at the bottom of each glass lantern through which a dim glimmer of light could just be discerned.

Sources for Chapter Four

43. *The Railway Times,*
44. *The Railway Magazine*, April 1910.
45. *Ibid.* September 1919.
46. *Ibid.* March 1931.
47. *Ibid.*

Blisworth station, seen here from the station approach, around 1950. This unusual building consisted of a central block flanked by two smaller extensions; items of interest include the letter box and window boxes.   *Lens of Sutton*

The LNWR station at Blisworth looking north, with the N&BJR just visible to the left. The up and down platform were linked by a subway which extended into the adjacent Northampton and Banbury Junction station.   *Mowat Collection*

A platform view of Blisworth N&BJ station. An 0–6–0 tender locomotive can be glimpsed at the head of its single coach train, while a spare passenger vehicle is stabled in the foreground; a class '8F' 2–8–0 stands on the adjacent main line. Photographed on 15th February, 1952. *H.C. Casserley*

Class '3F' 0–6–0 No. 43693 waits patiently in its platform at Blisworth, while luggage and bicycles are piled into the guard's compartment. Note the simple water column with its adjacent 'fire devil'. *Lens of Sutton*

Blisworth N&BJR station in the 1950s, with class '3F' 0−6−0 No. 43568 standing with a train for Stratford-upon-Avon. *H.C. Casserley*

Blisworth locomotive shed and signal box, photographed in the early 1930s. Note the 'interlaced turnout' in the foreground (i.e. a turnout incorporating several short sleepers instead of a smaller number of long timbers). Numerous chicken coops can be seen to the right, utilizing railway land! *D.S. Barrie*

Chapter Five

Along the Line from Blisworth to Banbury

Having examined the history of the Northampton & Banbury Junction line from its inception until World War II, it would now be convenient to study the route of this interesting railway in greater detail, and the following chapter will therefore take readers on an imaginary journey from Blisworth to Banbury Merton Street. The topographical details in this section will be based upon the line as it would have appeared around 1950.

Blisworth (SMJ)

Services commenced at Blisworth, where the station — used by trains to Stratford-upon-Avon as well as those to Banbury — was situated to the west of its London & North Western counterpart. The former Northampton & Banbury Junction station had just one island platform, though the presence of a 42 ft diameter engine turntable and an array of parallel goods sidings contributed an air of importance at this otherwise undistinguished place. There was, at one time, a small locomotive shed for S&MJ engines, but this modest structure was closed in 1929 and re-erected at Towcester, where it fulfilled a useful function as a store.

As mentioned earlier, the layout at Blisworth did not permit proper through running between the LNWR and S&MJ systems, and for this reason traffic was exchanged via the goods yard — a complicated and time-consuming procedure involving much shunting! For foot passengers, the process of changing stations was eased by the provision of a subway connection between the S&MJ station and LNWR down platform (though it is doubtful if this facility was fully appreciated by travellers burdened by heavy hand-luggage).

Although Blisworth was little more than a large, isolated village, it was, in former days, a place of considerable importance, being both a canal and a railway junction. Moreover, the Grand Union Canal was not entirely superseded by the London & Birmingham Railway, and in the Victorian period the village was something of an industrial centre, with several brickworks, limeworks and boat yards in the immediate vicinity.

In pre-grouping days the LNWR and S&MJ stations maintained separate staffing establishments, each station having its own station master. In the 1870s, the Northampton & Banbury Junction station master had been Edmund Stanton, but by 1890 Mr Stanton had been transferred to Towcester as "traffic superintendent" of the N&BJR, his place at Blisworth being taken by John Owen. A later station master, around 1906, was Harry Ashby, who was later transferred to Helmdon. In 1910 Blisworth's station master was Albert Gilkes, while in the years following World War I the station master here was Frederick William Parker.

The Northampton & Banbury Junction terminus was situated in the backyard of the LNWR station. It was very much a "poor relation" that seemed to be hiding from its mighty neighbours; the main station building was simple to the point of austerity, and its severe brick facade resembled the kind of non-conformist chapels once found in the back streets of English provincial towns. The main block was attached to two smaller wings which flanked the platform, while waiting travellers were shielded from the elements by a simple "umbrella" type canopy.

The operational side of the station was as basic as the terminal buildings; neither of the platform roads was equipped with a run-round loop, and for this reason newly-arrived trains had to reverse back towards Towcester once their passengers had disembarked, in order that locomotives could run-round.

A small goods yard was located on the down side of the London & North Western station, and additional cattle pens and loading facilities were provided beside one of the N&BJ passenger roads. Other goods or storage sidings were situated between the N&BJ and LNWR lines, in which position they could be used for inter-change purposes (but not for loading or unloading).

A simple hydrant-type water column was strategically positioned at the end of the platform, and this facility enabled locomotives to replenish their tenders prior to setting off on the journey to Banbury (or Stratford). Nearby, a rectangular water tank stood on four brick "stilts"; an attached pipe and flexible hose was available for tender-filling purposes. Other facilities at the Northampton & Banbury Junction station included a gabled wooden signal cabin and a tiny ground frame from which the siding connections to the LNWR were controlled.

Towcester

Leaving Blisworth, trains immediately swung south-westwards in a great arc and after a brief ascent at 1 in 553, the single line commenced its climb towards Tiffield summit. With the sharp exhaust of the labouring engine leaving no doubt that the general direction was now uphill, the climb steepened to 1 in 71, until, after about one and a half miles, the route started to drop down to the Tove Valley at 1 in 75.

Coasting downhill, trains rattled past the tiny village of Tiffield, where, from 1869 until 1871, there had been a small "conditional stop" station. The term "halt" did not come into general usage until the turn-of-the-century, but it seems that Tiffield had been a sort of temporary stopping place with minimal facilities (in other words a halt in all but name). Beyond, the route levelled-out for a short distance before resuming its descent towards Towcester on falling gradients of 1 in 75.

With a minor road running parallel to the left, the former Northampton & Banbury Junction line approached the important intermediate station of Towcester. Still falling at 1 in 75, the railway entered Towcester from the north-east, the line through the station being double tracked in order to accommodate traffic from the Stratford-upon-Avon, Towcester & Midland Junction Railway, which converged with the Blisworth line about a quarter of a mile to the east of the platforms at "Olney Branch Junction".

Situated some 4 miles 15 chains from Blisworth, Towcester had three platform faces, the main station building being on the up side. Of brick construction, it was a gabled structure of two stories; a small. platform canopy projected from the front of the building, and there were single storey extensions on either side of the main two storey block. Internally, the station provided the usual booking office, waiting room, and toilet facilities,

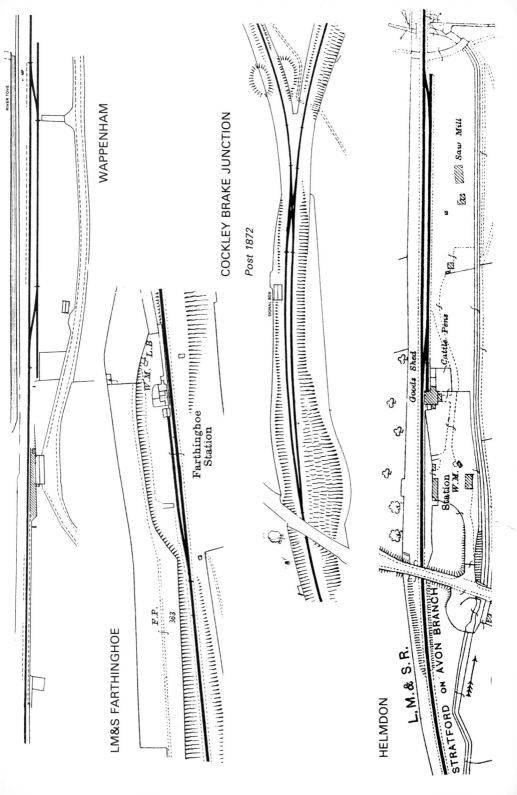

LM&S FARTHINGHOE

WAPPENHAM

RIVER TOVE

COCKLEY BRAKE JUNCTION

Post 1872

SIGNAL BOX

W.M. L.B

F.P.

363

Farthinghoe
Station

HELMDON

L. M. & S. R.

STRATFORD on AVON BRANCH

Goods Shed

Cattle Pens

Saw Mill

Station
W.M.

A 'mixed' train stands in the up platform at Towcester in the 1930s; the train apparently consists of a bogie coach, two 6-wheelers, a GWR cattle wagon and at least four open vehicles.   *Douglas Thompson*

A much earlier view, showing Towcester station at the turn-of-the century; the footbridge and downside waiting shelter were later replaced, while the vertical fencing along the rear of the up platform was subsequently replaced by Midland-style fencing as shown in other photographs. The tall signal box has not yet been installed.
Lens of Sutton

A view looking west from the footbridge at Towcester station in 1933. The A5 road bridge can be discerned in the distance, while the turntable is visible to the left of the 4-doll down starter signals. *Mowat Collection*

A rear view of Towcester station showing the solid brick façade that was in effect, a 2-storey version of Blisworth station. The Elizabeth II Coronation poster suggests that this photograph was taken in 1953. *Lens of Sutton*

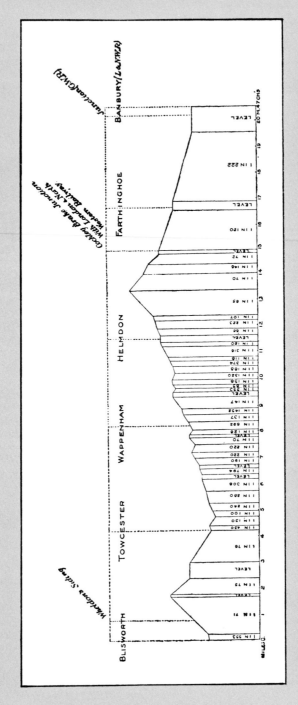

Gradient profile of the Northampton & Banbury Junction line. Note that the route was generally uphill between Towcester and Helmdon, the steepest section being 1 in 65 in the 'Cotswold' area beyond Helmdon station.

together with living accommodation for the station master and his family.

A substantial footbridge linked the up and down platforms, and there was a reasonably-spacious goods yard on the down side. Other facilities at this attractive country station included a 42 ft diameter turntable (useful when large engines traversed the line in connection with Towcester races), a gabled signal cabin, and an assortment of small permanent way huts. Prior to 1929 there had also been a small, single-road locomotive shed, but this facility was subsequently taken out of use.

Towcester's signal cabin was situated immediately to the east of the down platform, resulting in something of a problem in that the nearby footbridge would have obstructed the view from a normal two-storey box. For this reason the station was provided with an unusually-tall three storey cabin in an attempt to secure an unimpeded view over the bridge. The box was not as venerable as it looked, and although of traditional appearance, it was erected in the early years of the present century as a replacement for an earlier signal cabin that had been sited further to the east. The glazed upper storey was "jetted" out over the down main line, and photographic evidence suggests that, when first built, its lower storey had been a stilted structure without timber cladding (latterly, however, the exposed wooden "legs" were sheeted-over in corrugated iron).

Internally, Towcester signal box was kept in pristine condition, with a highly polished linoleum floor and spotlessly-clean windows. As usual in old style signal boxes, the brightly coloured point and signal levers had burnished metal handles, and signalmen worked the lever frame with the aid of small cloths or dusters that would not blemish the shining metalwork.

It is believed that the signal box incorporated prefabricated wooden components supplied by the Gloucester Wagon Company, and in this context it is interesting to note that the box featured tiny, rectangular windows high in its gables, similar to those found on many other GWCo boxes. (It is known that the Northampton & Banbury Junction Railway purchased a quantity of equipment from the Gloucester Wagon Company in the 1880s, and some of these components may have been re-used when Towcester signal box was rebuilt prior to World War I.)

In contrast to the signal box, Towcester goods shed was an entirely conventional structure. Of brick construction, it contained an internal loading platform, and the main goods office was housed in a single storey extension that extended from the west wall; a similar, but somewhat smaller extension projected from the eastern end of the main structure.

Until 1893, Towcester had served as a junction station for branch services to Olney, as well as an interchange point for Blisworth–Banbury and Blisworth–Stratford-upon-Avon services. Olney trains usually ran into the station four times each day in order to provide connections with the East & West Junction services to Stratford.

Like other rural stations, Towcester was a significant employment centre in an otherwise agricultural area, and in addition to directly-employed porters, signalmen, booking clerks, goods clerks and permanent way men, the station created indirect employment for a variety of non-railway or contract workers including coal men, carriers and draymen. In 1890, for instance, local trade directories reveal that the parcels carrying agency was held by Robert Austin, while Isaac Marlow was the "goods carrying agent"; Mr Marlow, a carrier, also provided road feeder services to Northampton on Mondays, Wednesdays and Saturdays.

The station master around 1870 was Frederick Bell Venner, but he was replaced by John Owen in about 1890, and Mr Owen was himself replaced by Thomas Holton in the Edwardian period. Curiously, Thomas Holton was subsequently moved to the much smaller station of Wappenham (a considerable drop in status that must have caused much resentment at the time). It is likely that this apparent demotion was connected with the 1910 amalgamation — a possible explanation being that when the N&BJR joined the Stratford-upon-Avon & Midland Junction Railway, Mr Holton was obliged to relinquish his post so that a long-serving East & West Junction employee could be promoted (Towcester was, after all, an important station on the enlarged S&MJ system).

Towcester's station master in the years following World War I was William Leigh, but sadly, Mr Leigh was forced to retire as a result of ill health in October 1929, and he died a few months later at the early age of 61.

As mentioned earlier, Towcester was, in N&BJ days, considered important enough to house the office of a traffic superintendent, and this position was filled for many years by Edmund Stanton, the former Blisworth station master. The traffic superintendent was of course a senior position, and one feels that N&BJ station masters must have felt rather uncomfortable to have this senior management figure in residence at their own station!

Towcester itself could be seen to the south of the railway. A small place, with little more than 2000 inhabitants, the town could trace its origins back to Roman times. Straddling historic Watling Street (the present A5) Towcester had once been an important coaching town, and in the 18th century many local people had found employment as innkeepers, ostlers, chamber maids or cooks. Sadly, the growth of railways elsewhere in the country destroyed Towcester's once lucrative coaching trade, and thereafter the town lapsed into a picturesque obscurity that lasted until the revival of road transport in the 1930s. Interestingly, Towcester was said to have been the inspiration for "Eatanswill" in Charles Dickens's *Pickwick Papers*, and there were also associations with Jonathan Swift (1667–1745), the author of *Gulliver's Travels*.

Inquisitive travellers, knowing that Towcester had been a Roman settlement, looked in vain for some sign of historic *Lactodorum*, but apart from some barely-discernible earthworks, there were few traces of the Roman town on the banks of the River Tove. The most obvious relic of Roman occupation was Watling Street itself — a broad highway running in a more or less dead straight line to the north and south of the modern town.

Leaving Towcester station, trains crossed the A5 on a substantial girder bridge, and with the red brick town visible to the left, the railway was carried through verdant water meadows on a low embankment. After about a quarter-of-a-mile, the line crossed the sparkling River Tove on a twin-span girder bridge resting on stone piers, and with the river running parallel to the north, down trains approached Greens Norton Junction.

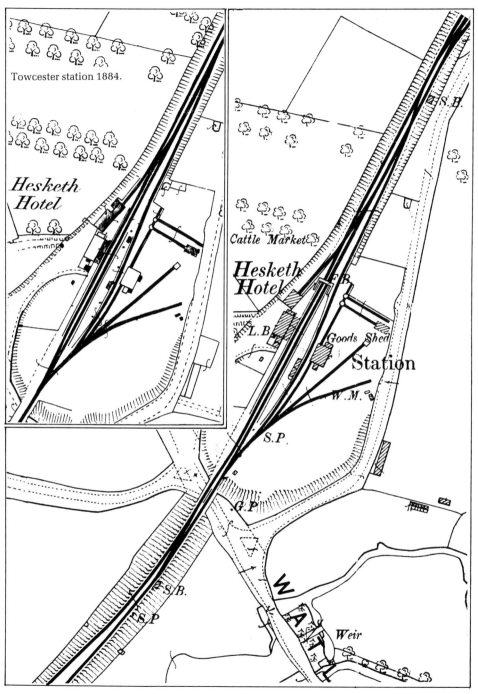

Towcester station 1884.

Hesketh
Hotel

Cattle Market

Hesketh
Hotel

L.B.

Goods Shed

Station

W.M.

S.P.

G.P.

S.B.

S.P.

WA

Weir

S.B.

Towcester station 1906. *Reproduced from the 25″, 1900 Ordnance Survey Map. The* insert (*top*) shows Towcester station c.1884.

A post-closure scene at Towcester, after removal of the canopies and downside buildings; this picture nevertheless provides a clear view of the station façade, that would otherwise have been hidden. *Lens of Sutton*

A view from a train on 15th March, 1952 provides many interesting details of the down platform at Towcester; note the characteristic LMS 'Hawkseye' type nameboard. The small waiting room was then being used by the P-Way Department.

H.C. Casserley

The platform ends at Towcester, showing the somewhat unusually tall signal cabin, which was designed to give an unobstructed view over the adjacent footbridge. Note the water column (*left*) a simple hydrant-type without a rotating boom. Modern upper quadrant signals have replaced the picturesque lower quadrants seen in some of the other photographs.   *Lens of Sutton*

Another general view showing Towcester in the 1930s, and providing useful details of the goods shed.   *Lens of Sutton*

A panoramic view of the eastern end of Towcester station. Spare coaches occupy the former engine shed siding (*right*) and an 0–6–0 tender engine can be seen in the up platform.   *L.G.R.P. Collection*

The junction at the east end of Towcester Station; the line from Blisworth trails in from the left while the Olney route disappears beneath the distant overbridge.
                                                                L.G.R.P. Collection

Until the early 1900s, the railway had been single tracked at this point, but after the 1910 amalgamation the S&MJ remodelled the western exit from Towcester to provide two single lines for Banbury and Stratford-upon-Avon traffic. To the layman, the resulting double-track configuation appeared to be a conventional double track, but in reality the two lines were signalled for bi-directional working and there was no physical connection at Greens Norton "junction", where the Stratford-upon-Avon route diverged north westwards.

Wappenham

Continuing south-westwards, the Banbury line commenced its long climb towards Helmdon summit — however, the gradients on this initial section were relatively easy, and after a brief stretch at 1 in 100, the climb eased to 1 in 240 and then 1 in 280. Crossing the River Tove for a second time since leaving Towcester, the single track railway soon entered a landscape with a character different to that encountered earlier. With the ascent averaging about 1 in 200, trains entered an area of rolling upland that was, in effect, an extension of the neighbouring Cotswold hills, and discerning travellers noted that the surrounding farms and villages were built of attractive, locally-quarried stone.

Entering a deep, wooded cutting, the wheezing LMS 0–6–0s and their short trains of maroon coaches rumbled beneath an overbridge carrying a minor road from Blakesley to Olney, and the line then emerged to cross the River Tove for a third time. Running along an embankment, the line passed between the villages of Slapton and Abthorpe, and with the meandering river still visible to the right, trains passed beneath another road overbridge before coming to a stand in an isolated, wayside station known — perhaps misleadingly — as Wappenham.

Situated some 8 miles 7 chains from Blisworth, Wappenham was over a mile from Wappenham village, but this apparently inconvenient location enabled it to serve as a useful railhead, not only for Wappenham but also for the neighbouring settlements of Slapton and Abthorpe. Facilities here were simple, and the station consisted of little more than a platform on the down side, with a single siding goods yard to the east. The siding was linked to the running line at each end to form a loop, and this arrangement enabled the yard to be shunted by either up or down goods trains. No goods shed was provided, but Wappenham's modest goods facilities were more than adequate to serve the needs of local farmers or traders; the types of traffic handled included coal inwards and agricultural produce outwards.

It is interesting to find that the stylish, red brick station building at Wappenham was similar to its counterparts on other lines engineered by Edward Richards. Indeed, the small rectangular structure was virtually the same as Alvescot, Fairford, and neighbouring stations on the East Gloucestershire line — the most obvious difference between the EGR and N&BJR buildings being that the latter had gabled (as opposed to half-hipped) roof structures.

Viewed from the platform, Wappenham station building was a symmetrical structure with a centrally-placed door that gave access to the waiting room; the ladies waiting room was situated to the right of the waiting room, while the ticket office and parcels offices were to the left. A wooden lean-to provided additional staff/parcels accommodation at the extreme eastern end of the building, while the gentlemens' urinal occupied a corresponding extension at the opposite end of the main block. Internally, the basic shell was sub-divided by transverse walling, and these dividing walls provided a firm support for two huge brick chimneys that rose through the roof in spectacular fashion. The staff accommodation at the east end of the building was provided with its own door from the platform, and the main public entrance was covered by a small projecting porch.

Wappenham was not a block post, and no signal box was needed, though there was space for a second platform and passing loop if traffic had justified such a facility. Significantly, the overbridge at the eastern end of the station had a "spare" arch which would have accommodated a second line of rails if doubling had ever been carried out.

Minor details at this extremely rural station included a loading dock for machinery and vehicular traffic, and a small weigh-house containing the usual Pooley weighing equipment. The platform was fenced (after 1910) with Midland-style "diagonal" paling, and illuminated by simple oil lamps housed in tapering glass lanterns. In summertime, the station was the setting for some colourful floral displays, its homely window boxes being a particularly attractive feature.

It appears that, when first opened, Wappenham had been deemed important enough to have its own station master, and *Whellan's Directory of Northamptonshire* reveals that the station master, in 1874, had been Joseph Pinfold; in fact, there were two N&BJR officials at Wappenham at that time — the above-mentioned Mr Pinfold and a man called Samuel Atterbury, who was described as a "permanent way inspector". In later years, Wappenham was supervised from nearby Helmdon, the idea being that both places would share the same station master; in 1910, for instance, Harry Ashby, the Helmdon station master, was officially described as the "collector" for Wappenham. At the Grouping, however, there seems to have been a change of heart vis-à-vis separate station masters, and (as we have seen) Thomas Holton, who had hitherto served at the more important station of Towcester, had been moved to Wappenham by 1924.

From Wappenham, the single line continued due westwards, and, climbing on gradients of 1 in 137 and 1 in 147, trains ran through fields which still bore the curious, corrugated imprint of Medieval ploughlands. Passing beneath a substantial triple arched bridge that carried nothing more than a farm track across the line, the route emerged from a shallow cutting; away to the left, the attractive, hilltop village of Wappenham could be seen clustered around its embattled church tower, while, in the foreground, a branch of the River Tove meandered peacefully between pollarded willows.

Curving imperceptibly onto a south-westerly heading, the railway passed under an overbridge carrying the lane from Wappenham to Weedon Lois over the line. Like other Northampton & Banbury Junction bridges, the Wappenham bridge was wide enough to accommodate a double track; a single span structure, it incorporated brick abutments and flimsy-looking

Wappenham station looking east towards Blisworth during the early 1930s. Designed by Edward Richards, the station building was similar to Richards' stone-built stations on the neighbouring GWR Fairford branch; note the window boxes. *Mowat Collection*

Ex-Midland Railway '4F' 0–6–0, No. 43873 pauses at Wappenham station on 29th June, 1951. The 'Hawkseye' pattern nameboard (*left*) can be seen to advantage.

John Edgington

Helmdon station seen from the adjacent overbridge, c.1930. Note the attractive floral displays on the platforms and on the embankment; the name 'HELMDON' is prominently displayed on the left, and the compact weigh-house is visible to the right of the station building.

Mowat Collection

wooden parapets. Beyond, the line crossed the River Tove for the fourth time since Towcester, and with the little river now visible on the right hand side, trains rounded a great curve as they continued their long ascent towards Helmdon.

Helmdon

Leaving the Tove valley, the route followed a small tributary stream for the next two miles, and this new course brought the route back onto a westerly heading. Still climbing, down trains rumbled beneath a further road overbridge which carried the road from Wappenham to Helmdon over the railway. Of brick and stone construction, this bridge was a twin-arch design, although of course only one arch was used by the single track Northampton & Banbury Junction line.

As their train emerged from under the bridge, travellers could, by glancing to the left, obtain a good view of "Astwell Castle" — a curious fortified tower standing, somewhat incongruously, in the middle of an otherwise undistinguished farmyard. Looking for all intents and purposes like a Northern Peel tower that had, by some historical accident, been erected in Northamptonshire rather than the Scottish borders, Astwell Castle (or manor) was merely a fragment of a much larger fortress. Yet it was of considerable interest in that it had been the birthplace of Selina, Countess of Huntingdon, (1707–91) the founder of an extreme Protestant sect known as "Lady Huntingdon's Connection"; at its peak, this Calvinistic sect encompassed over sixty churches!

Continuing its ascent, the railway passed through a tract of pleasant, rolling countryside before eventually reaching Helmdon, where clusters of attractive limestone houses imparted a distinct "Cotswold" atmosphere to this Northamptonshire village. Situated 11 miles 59 chains from Blisworth, Helmdon station occupied a shallow cutting that was spanned, at its western end, by another twin-arched road overbridge carrying the village street across the railway. The bridge was constructed of what appeared to be a random mixture of local stone and engineer's blue brickwork — suggesting that the structure had been extensively rebuilt on more than one occasion!

The station was generally similar to Wappenham, and the track plan again consisted of a single loop siding, with short spurs at each end. Unlike Wappenham, Helmdon was provided with a small, red brick goods shed, of similar design (though smaller) than the shed at Towcester. A conventional gabled structure, Helmdon goods shed spanned the goods siding, and the cart entrance in its south wall was partially covered by a projecting canopy; a goods office abutted the eastern wall, and an internal loading platform facilitated the transfer of goods between rail and road vehicles.

In operational terms, Helmdon was of more importance than Wappenham in that it was originally a block post; in later years, however, the line was worked as one staff section from Towcester to Cockley Brake, and Helmdon lost its former importance as a staff station.

Architecturally, Helmdon station mirrored neighbouring Wappenham, and the single storey, red brick station building was another typical E. Richards' design incorporating a parcels/booking office and waiting room, together with a ladies room and toilet facilities. This attractive Victorian structure stood on a single platform, but there was ample room for a second platform on the opposite side of the line. Other facilities at Helmdon included the usual cattle dock, loading bay, and weigh-house, together with a fixed hand crane of 1 ton 10 cwt. capacity. The weigh-house was a small, gabled building with a large window in its front wall and a door at the side; like the nearby station building, this humble structure was a standard "Richards" design, and identical buildings could be found at Alvescot, Fairford and other stations engineered by Edward Richards in the 1870s.

One of Helmdon's first station masters was Charles Stevens, but he was later replaced by George Brown — who remained in charge of both Helmdon and Wappenham until about 1908; thereafter, the station was supervised by Harry Ashby, who had formerly served at Blisworth. Mr Ashby was himself replaced in the years following World War I, and the station master here at the time of the Grouping was Mr Frederick Smart.

Although merely an unimportant village, Helmdon enjoyed ample rail transport facilities, and in addition to the Northampton & Banbury Junction station this tiny place was also served by the Great Central Railway; the latter company's station was, however, less favourably sited than the N&BJR establishment, being inconveniently situated at the southern end of the village.

Leaving Helmdon, westbound trains passed beneath the above-mentioned brick and stone overbridge, and, rounding a gentle curve, accelerated towards the Great Central main line. Running from north to south, this important trunk route was carried high above the N&BJR line on a soaring, arched viaduct with nine 34 ft brick spans. Like most engineering structures on the GCR London extension, Helmdon viaduct was solidly constructed of blue-grey brickwork, which contrasted favourably with the surrounding lime-stone villages and farmsteads.

Having passed beneath the Great Central main line, the N&BJR line approached its summit, and turning south-westwards once more, the railway climbed at 1 in 65 as it surmounted a 550 ft ridge of Oolitic limestone. With Cotswold-like hills visible on either side, trains laboured past the deserted Medieval village of Stuchbury — though little remained above ground to mark the site of this abandoned settlement. A short distance beyond, the route skirted the still-extant village of Greatworth which, like Helmdon, was a picturesque, Cotswold stone settlement with many interesting old houses. Here, in the early 1500s, had lived Amy Pargiter, who was destined, in later years, to marry Lawrence Washington of Sulgrave (1500–84), an ancestor of President George Washington.

Cockley Brake Junction

Coasting downhill, Banbury-bound trains followed a long, curving embankment and with the falling gradient steepening to 1 in 72, the route approached its junction with the LNWR Buckinghamshire branch at Cockley Brake Junction. Slowing for the compulsory exchange of train staffs at Cockley Brake signal box, down workings passed over a minor road on a

A general view of the classic 'Edward Richards' type station building at Helmdon; the blacked-out platform lamps and blank nameboard show that this photograph was taken during World War II. *Lens of Sutton*

The standard LNWR signal box at Cockley Brake was a typical twentieth century North Western box, with the slightly over-hanging roof introduced at the turn-of-the-century. Photographed on 15th March, 1955. *R.M. Casserley*

A general view of Cockley Brake Junction probably taken around 1930; LNWR signalling equipment is again much in evidence. *Mowat Collection*

The converging lines at Cockley Brake Junction, showing the N&BJR (*left*) and the
LNWR Buckinghamshire branch (*right*). Standard LNWR semaphores control the
N&BJ line but the tall signal visible on the extreme right has been fitted with a modern
upper quadrant arm. *L.G.R.P. Collection*

small bridge before the two lines converged in a shallow cutting to the north of Cockley Hill Farm.

The layout at Cockley Brake was more complex than one might have expected, and although a simple single track junction would have sufficed at this bucolic location, a double track intersection was provided; the N&BJ line doubled before converging with the Buckinghamshire branch, and westbound trains crossed the up "main line" on the level before entering the down loop. This comparatively complicated junction was controlled from a standard London & North Western signal cabin that had replaced an earlier hip-roofed box around 1920. Of brick and timber construction, the new box was a 3-bay structure with the characteristic "wide" eaves introduced on LNWR boxes in the 20th century (earlier, 19th century boxes were distinguished by their somewhat slab-sided appearance).

Cockley Brake box was manned by two L&NW signalmen who worked overlapping shifts. The longest-serving employee here was Henry Somerton, and he worked at Cockley Brake from 1903 until the end of World War II; his colleague, from 1901 until 1922, was Mr Bird, who died in 1939 at the age of 82 years.

Farthinghoe

From Cockley Brake the single line continued south-westwards on a 1 in 180 falling gradient. Running first in cuttings and then on an embankment, the railway was carried across the busy A422 Brackley to Banbury road on an arched viaduct before trains shuddered to a stand beside the ramshackle wooden platform at Farthinghoe station.

A tiny place, Farthinghoe was 16 miles 50 chains from Blisworth, and it consisted of little more than a single platform and a solitary goods siding on the up side of the line. The most interesting feature here was undoubtedly the station building — a complex structure built partly of timber and partly of brick. The main ticket office and booking hall occupied a single-storey, weather boarded wing with a steeply-pitched gable roof that projected over the platform in lieu of a proper canopy. An adjacent two-storey brick wing incorporated domestic accommodation for the local station master, and these two disparate sections were physically linked by a two-storey, tile-hung central block containing a waiting room and other accommodation. This central block was arranged at right angles to the two cross wings, and the resulting structure was therefore built to a sort of 'H' plan. However, the domestic block and the waiting room section were set well back from the platform, and the station's interior layout was further obscured by an extension of the wooden booking hall, through which travellers passed to enter the waiting room.

It remains a matter of conjecture why the Buckinghamshire Railway should have erected such an unusual structure, but a clue can be found in the half-year report for the six months ending in June 1848. That document (referred to in Chapter One) reveals that, in view of an underlying economic crisis, the Directors had decided to spend less money on their stations, and whereas some Buckinghamshire Railway structures were substantially built of Cotswold stone, stations at the western extremities of the system (i.e. the

Farthinghoe station looking west towards Banbury, in early LMS days. Items of interest include the low wooden platform and standard LNWR fencing. Four open wagons occupy the single siding goods yard.

Mowat Collection

Farthinghoe from the west, showing the station master's accommodation (18th March, 1955).   *R.M. Casserley*

A close-up of the unusual wood-and-brick station building at Farthinghoe station which was formed of three separate but inter-connected portions.   *Lens of Sutton*

last to be built) were constructed mainly of timber. To Victorian eyes, such buildings must have seemed hideously plain, but modern travellers would have been charmed by the delightful "Emmett"-like atmosphere that lingered for so long at Farthinghoe.

Farthinghoe's goods facilities were extremely limited, and the single dead-end siding could be used only by down trains, which were able to set back after drawing forwards clear of the points. The traffic handled here was inevitably of an agricultural nature, consisting mainly of cattle, milk and animal feed. There was a small amount of incoming coal traffic for Palmers, the local coal merchants.

Other facilities at Farthinghoe included a cattle dock, a weigh-house, a platelayers' hut and a lamp hut; the platform was fenced with typical LNWR wooden fencing, and the ornate glass lanterns were more decorative than those normally provided at North Western country stations. The name FARTHINGHOE was originally displayed on a single wooden nameboard, but standard LMS "Hawkseye" nameplates were erected on the eve of World War II; these signs were four feet long, and supported by a creosoted wooden framing.

Although only a minor stopping place, Farthinghoe had its own station master in the person of William Tustain, who supervised the station for several years of the present century. Mr Tustain remained in office until World War I, but he was subsequently replaced by John Harris. Another employee at Farthinghoe was lad porter Harold Chester, who assisted Mr Tustain around 1913. In its declining years, the station was staffed by just one man, who lived in the station house and was known locally as "the station master", although he was, in reality, a porter.

Departing from Farthinghoe, trains passed beneath an overbridge carrying a minor road across the line, and, falling steadily, the route continued due west towards the Oxfordshire border. Running first in cuttings, and then on embankments, the railway traversed a prosperous agricultural area, and discriminating travellers were treated to many tantalising glimpses of a landscape shaped and moulded by centuries of continuous cultivation.

Banbury Merton Street

Passing under two more overbridges, the route emerged onto a further stretch of embankment which was pierced, at one point, by an underbridge. To the north, the remote village of Warkworth was another "Cotswold" type settlement with a curiously-isolated church standing in a field; this village was devastated by a major fire in 1811, when many of its thatched houses were destroyed.

Westwards, the line continued towards Warkworth Crossing, with its typical crossing keeper's cottage. There was, at one time, an extensive munitions factory in the immediate vicinity, and an area of land to the north of Warkworth Crossing was formerly occupied by an array of exchange sidings. Opened in World War I, "Banbury Munitions Factory" specialised in the manufacture of all kinds of projectiles including mines, depth charges and artillery shells. At its peak, the establishment employed about 2000 people, many of them female shell-fillers. The factory was served by a network of standard gauge and narrow gauge lines, and at least one 0−6−0 saddle tank was used for internal shunting work. North Western trains were permitted to enter the exchange sidings, the points giving access from the "main line" being actuated by the Banbury to Cockley Brake electric train staff. There was no signal box at the junction, and this obviously presented problems in terms of train staff retrieval; to overcome this problem, the single line staff was handed to a guard or shunter after trains had entered the sidings, and this unfortunate individual proceeded on foot to Banbury signal box, so that the staff could be handed over to the duty signalman. When the train was ready to leave the munitions siding, the signalman handed another staff to the guard or shunter, who then returned to the siding with the staff so that the train could continue its journey.

The Banbury Munitions Factory remained in use for a few years after World War I, albeit for the "breaking down" or destruction of munitions rather than manufacturing purposes. These activities continued until the early 1920s, but thereafter the factory was closed completely, and the Warkworth site returned to nature.

From Warkworth, the single line maintained its westerly heading, and, still descending, trains approached their destination. Nearing Banbury, the railway crossed the county boundary between Northamptonshire and Oxfordshire, and with the Great Western main line now visible to the left, the twenty mile journey from Blisworth drew to a close. Slowing to walking pace, trains passed Banbury Gas Works, and finally entered the wooden island platform at Banbury Merton Street; here, in a small terminus, 20 miles 43 chains from Blisworth, Northampton & Banbury Junction trains came to a stand beneath a miniature overall roof.

Banbury Merton Street was similar, in many ways, to Oxford Rewley Road (at the end of the Buckinghamshire Railway's Oxford branch) and both stations featured a simple, island layout, with wooden buildings situated at right angles to the terminal buffers. At Banbury, the buildings were of distinctive "Great Western" appearance, with arched windows and doorways recalling contemporary "Brunel" style stations such as Charlbury or Evesham (old) station. It is possible that Merton Street incorporated pre-fabricated timber components purchased from the GWR, but, perhaps more likely, the station may have been fabricated with the aid of standardised timber panels supplied by some external builder. It is known, for example, that the Witney builder Malachi Bartlett (1802−75) carried out railway contracts at Banbury — although this work took place several years *after* the line's opening.

The station's trackplan incorporated dead-end passenger roads on either side of the island platform, the northernmost road (used by N&BJR trains) having its own run-round facility whereas the opposite side was a simple, dead-end bay; trains using the latter platform had to reverse into a run-round loop situated to the south of the passenger station after travellers had alighted. The northern end of the wooden platform was protected by a semi-circular roof spanning both tracks and there was a small circulating area in front of the station building.

Goods facilities were spread out on both sides of the passenger station, the main goods shed and loading area being to the west, while the station's

The single wooden platform at Banbury Merton Street, seen here in the early 1930s. Cattle wagons are much in evidence suggesting that the photograph may have been taken on market day. Note that the wooden platform had a short brick-built section (by the second lamp-post) — this marked the site of a transfer siding which linked most of the station's terminal roads and was entered via a series of wagon turntables.

L.G.R.P. Collection

Banbury Merton Street from the station forecourt in early British Railways' days. The arched windows recall contemporary Great Western practice, suggesting that the wooden station building incorporated pre-fabricated components from some local supplier (who may also have carried out joinery for the GWR). The tall chimneys were later cut down. *L.G.R.P. Collection*

A view of Merton Street after it was repainted in the mid-1950s. The tall metal chimney visible to the right was probably connected to a furnace used to supply hot water (or heat cinders for old-fashioned foot warmers). *Brian Leslie*

extensive cattle pens occupied a corresponding position on the eastern side of the line. Coal (and other types of bulk wagon load traffic) was handled in two long sidings near the goods shed, and there were additional facilities for the loading and unloading of vehicles or heavy machinery beside the cattle pens on the up side of the line. One of the down side sidings continued, beyond the limits of LNWR property, to form a useful connection to the adjacent Great Western station, while a further connecting line diverged from the North Western line in order to serve the Banbury Gas Company. This private siding formed an end-on connection with a Great Western siding — although the resulting LNWR–GWR link was hardly suitable for through running.

The adjacent Great Western station was slightly younger than its LNWR neighbour, having opened to traffic on Monday 2nd September, 1850, when trains commenced running between Oxford and Banbury. It was, at that time, little more than a branch terminus, but when the GWR route was extended northwards to Birmingham in 1852, the Great Western station was elevated to main line status. Always a more important station than the nearby LNWR establishment, the GWR station was regarded as an important transport facility and when, in the 1930s, the LMS and GWR companies decided to build a new joint station, they agreed that Merton Street would be closed, enabling passenger services to be diverted into the Great Western platforms. Unfortunately, World War II intervened before this scheme could be brought to fruition, and when BR opened a new, five-platform station in 1958, it was used only by main line services.

In the meantime, Banbury Merton Street had already been down-graded. Its large goods shed, for example, was demolished in the 1930s, while the former North Western engine shed was closed in 1934 — though turning and stabling facilities remained *in situ*.

Banbury itself could be seen to the north and west of the station, but there was little for inquisitive visitors to see. Much of the town was Victorian — including the famous "Banbury Cross" which was erected in 1859 in imitation of an original Eleanor Cross. In earlier times, the town had boasted several interesting old buildings (including a castle and various picturesque old inns) but most of these structures were swept away in the 17th and 18th centuries.

Apart from its nursery rhyme cross, Banbury was famous for its "Banbury Cakes" which were aptly described, by Edwardian editions of *The Little Guide to Oxfordshire*, as "a sort of compromise between a tart and a mince-pie"; these distinctive cakes were, according to the Guide, "still industriously hawked at the neighbouring railway stations" in the early 1900s.

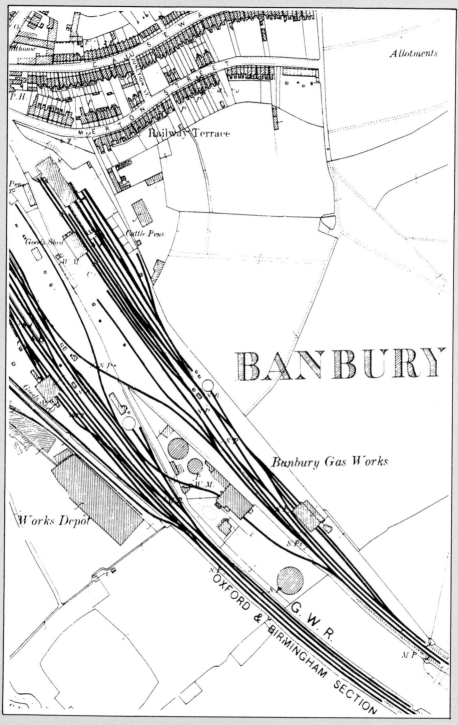

Reproduced from the 1900, 25″ Ordnance Survey Map

The train shed at Banbury station was removed after the withdrawal of N&BJR services, but this partial demolition did at least let more light into the circulating area — making photography possible! *Lens of Sutton*

The station throat in 1933; this photograph (apparently taken from a convenient signal post) shows the LNWR locomotive shed and the neighbouring gas works, through which a siding extended to form a connection to the GWR station. *Mowat Collection*

Class '4F', 0−6−0 No. 43873 waits in the island platform at Towcester on 29th June, 1951; the train is the 4.45 pm evening service from Banbury to Blisworth.

John Edgington

The 6.31 pm evening train from Blisworth to Banbury enters Towcester on 16th June, 1951. The engine is ex-Midland class '3F' 0−6−0, No. 43521, and the single coach is a standard LMS 57 ft non-corridor vehicle; unusually, the engine is running tender-first towards Banbury.

Ian L. Wright

A timeless scene at Wappenham station in June 1951 as class '3F' 0−6−0, No. 43694 stands beside the deserted platform with the 4.45 pm evening train from Banbury Merton Street.   *Ian L. Wright*

An atmospheric view taken inside Blisworth N&BJ station, on a sunny March day during the early British Railways' period; a shaft of sunlight has highlighted the roof structure, with its central king posts and horizontal tie beams.   *H.C. Casserley*

Towcester station looking east, probably around 1948. A mixed freight stands in the up platform while, to the right, workmen are busy converting the down side station building into an office for the PW Inspector. The brick-built goods shed is prominent to the right.

Lens of Sutton

Table 266   BROOM JUNCTION, STRATFORD-ON-AVON, BANBURY, and BLISWORTH
(One class only)

		Week Days only								Miles from Blisworth		Week Days only					
Miles from Broom Jc.		a.m	a.m	a.m	p.m	p.m	p.m	p.m	p.m			a.m	a.m	a.m		a.m	p.m	pm	pm
	210 GLOUCESTER 263 .. dep	..	..	..	..	..	..	..			50 London (Euston).. dep	6 50	..	11 37	11 37	4 30	..
	210 CHELTENHAM A 263 „	..	..	..	..	..	..	..			70 NORTHAMPTON (C.). „	8 23	9 0	1 30	2 32	5 32	..
	263 BIRMINGHAM B .. „	..	..	..	..	..	..	..		4½	Blisworth .... dep	8 50	9 31	2 0	4 0	5 0	636
	Broom Junction ... dep	..	..	..	..	..	..	..			Towcester .... arr	8 59	9 40	2 9	4 10	5 9	645
1½	Bidford-on-Avon	..	..	..	..	..	..	..			Towcester .... dep	..	9 41	..	..	6 10	..
2½	Binton	..	..	..	..	..	..	..		8½	Wappenham	..	9 51	..	..	6 22	..
7¼	Stratford-on-Avon { arr	..	..	..	..	..	..	..		12	Helmdon	..	10 0	..	..	6 32	..
	{ dep	7 43	..	1158	..	..	6 25	9 45	..	16½	Farthinghoe	..	1012	..	..	6 47	..
12½	Ettington	7 58	..	1211	..	..	6 38	9 58	..	20½	Banbury D ...... arr	..	1020	..	..	6 55	..
16¾	Kineton	8 6	..	1219	..	..	6 46	10 5	..		Towcester .... dep	9 0	..	2 10	4 15	..	646
23	Fenny Compton ...	8 20	..	1233	..	..	6 58	..	..	8½	Blakesley ....[grave	9 10	..	2 19	4 23	..	65½
30	Byfield .... arr	8 32	..	1245	..	..	7 10	..	..	11½	Morton Pinkney, for Sul-	9 20	..	2 26	4 30	..	7 1
32	Woodford C ... dep	..	..	..	..	..	7 18	..	..	15½	Byfield	9 32	..	2 33	4 39	..	7 9
10½	London (Mar.).. arr	..	..	..	..	..	7 23	..	..	17½	Byfield .... dep	..	..	..	..	..	7 18
	Woodford C ... dep	..	..	..	..	..	..	..	..		Woodford C ...... arr	..	..	..	..	..	723
	Byfield .... arr	..	..	..	..	..	9 34	..	..		London (Mar.) .. dep	..	..	..	..	..	6 5
34	Morton Pinkney, for Sul- dep	8 33	..	1246	4 45	..	7 11	..	..		Woodford C ...... dep	..	..	..	..	..	840
37½	Blakesley	8 43	..	1256	4 55	..	7 22	..	..		Byfield .... arr	..	..	..	..	..	846
41½	Towcester ...... arr	8 50	..	1 3	5 1	..	7 29	..	..	22½	Byfield .... dep	9 33	..	2 36	..	..	846
	{ arr	8 57	..	1 10	5 9	..	7 36	..	..	29	Fenny Compton ...	9 46	..	2 48	..	..	857
	M½ Banbury D ... dep	..	1040	..	..	4 45	..	..	..	33	Kineton	10 1	..	3 2	..	..	9 9
	4 Farthinghoe	..	1049	..	..	4 54	..	..	..	33	Ettington	1010	..	3 11	..	..	917
	8½ Helmdon	..	11 2	..	..	5 7	..	..	..	38½	Stratford-on- { arr	1021	..	3 22	..	..	926
	12½ Wappenham	..	1111	..	..	5 15	..	..	..		Avon { dep	..	..	..	..	..	..
	16½ Towcester .... arr	..	1120	..	..	5 22	..	..	..	42	Binton	..	..	..	..	..	..
	Towcester .... dep	9 2	1121	11 15	10	5 23	7 37	..	..	44½	Bidford-on-Avon	..	..	..	..	..	..
45½	Blisworth .... arr	9 12	1130	1 22	5 20	5 32	7 47	..	..	45½	Broom Junction ... arr	..	..	..	..	..	..
50½	70 NORTHAMPTON (C.) arr	9 35	12 02	8	..	6 1	8 9	..	..	71½	263 BIRMINGHAM B .. arr	..	..	..	..	..	..
108½	50 London (Euston).. „	1210	1 5	4 35	..	7 J45	11 J5	..	..	70½	210 CHELTENHAM A 263 „	..	..	..	..	..	..
										77½	210 GLOUCESTER 263 .. „	..	..	..	..	..	..

A Cheltenham Spa, Lansdown.   Å Arr. 9 16 a.m.   B New Street.   C Woodford & Hinton (E.R.).
D Merton Street.   J Via Northampton.   S Saturdays only.   U Arr. 5 mins. *earlier*.

For OTHER TRAINS between Banbury and Farthinghoe, see Table 66.

Bradshaw's passenger timetable for May 1948.

Class '3F' 0–6–0 No. 43568 simmers gently in the N&BJR station at Blisworth: the combination of ex-LMS 0–6–0 plus single brake 3rd was a characteristic sight on the former SMJ lines after World War II. The photograph was taken on 15th February, 1952 and the train is a Blisworth–Towcester–Stratford working.

H.C. Casserley

Chapter Six

The Final Years (1948–1967)

The end of the war in Europe was followed, on 26th July, 1945, by the election of a Labour government, pledged to nationalise rail transport and other important industries. The new administration lost no time in putting these radical ideas into effect, and at midnight on 31st December, 1947 a nationwide fanfare of locomotive whistles welcomed the demise of private ownership and the creation of a new, national railway organisation known as "British Railways".

In many places, a feeling of elation filled the air, but there were no special celebrations on the former Northampton & Banbury Junction line. In fact the immediate effects of nationalisation were remarkably few, and the only sign that a momentous change of ownership had taken place concerned the liveries of locomotives and rolling stock — though even this modest innovation took many months to fully implement, and the new liveries (black for mixed traffic or goods engines and maroon for non-corridor coaching stock) were similar to those previously employed by the now-defunct LMS. Similarly, unfitted goods vehicles were painted in a light grey colour scheme resembling that used by the LMS, while the choice of "bauxite" brown for fitted freight stock recalled a colour scheme used on the LMS after 1937. (Bauxite was, in theory, the standard LMS freight livery after 1937, but most LMS wagons were still painted grey at the start of World War II.)

Post-War Train Services

Post-war train services were very similar to those provided in the LMS era, with a basic weekday pattern of 2 up and 2 down trains between Blisworth and Banbury, augmented by 3 additional workings each way between Blisworth, Towcester and Stratford-upon-Avon.

In 1948, the first down train departed from Blisworth at 9.31 am, reaching Towcester about eight minutes later and arriving in Banbury at 10.20. Having run-round, the train returned from Banbury at 10.40 am and arrived back in Blisworth by 11.30. The second (and last) up train of the day left Banbury at 4.45 pm, and arrived in Blisworth at 5.32; finally, a balancing down service left Blisworth at 6.00 pm, and reached Banbury at 6.55.

This timetable had remained more or less unchanged for many years, apart from minor adjustments in the times of arrival and departure. The June 1950 timetable was identical to its 1948 predecessor, but small alterations had been introduced by the following year, and the 1951 passenger time-table shows the first train of the day departing from Blisworth at 9.16 am, and arriving in Banbury at 10.04. The return working still left Banbury at 10.40 am, but the evening down service from Blisworth left at the later time of 6.32 pm; the 4.45 pm up train was unaltered.

The line was still worked, in these last years, by ex-LMS '3F' or '4F' 0–6–0s, typical numbers, around 1950, being '3F' 0–6–0s Nos. 43520, 43568 and 43693, together with '4F' 0–6–0s Nos. 43873, 43876, 43886, 44204, 44242, 44524, 44525, 44567 and 44587. These relatively large loco-motives hauled trains which frequently consisted of just one coach con-taining no more than a handful of faithful passengers. It is interesting to note

Class '4F' 0−6−0, No. 43873 waits at Helmdon station with the evening train to Blisworth on 29th June, 1951. Note that the platform extended as far as the goods shed and thereby obstructed the large doors seen in the western gable (for this reason the siding that ran into the shed ended abruptly near the sloping platform ramp).

John Edgington

Ex-MR '3F' 0−6−0, No. 3529 stands in Helmdon station with a two coach train, in the years before World War II.

Lens of Sutton

that some Banbury to Blisworth trains were officially classified as "mixed" workings, and these services were permitted to convey goods vehicles in addition to their solitary passenger vehicle. The coaches used at this time were usually ex-LMS non-corridor 57 ft brake thirds — any first class compartments would have been superfluous because the line was "third class only". (One of the coaches seen around 1950 was No. M20264, a panelled vehicle that had been built at Newton Heath in 1927.)

In common with many other parts of the British railway system, the lines from Blisworth to Banbury and from Banbury to Verney Junction had been allowed to run-down through lack of maintenance during the 1939–45 war, and presumably for this reason the engine turntable at Banbury Merton Street became inoperable. Locomotive crews were, in consequence, authorised to use the nearby Western Region table but in practice the men often worked Blisworth services tender-first. It has been suggested that this curious reluctance to use WR facilities stemmed from the need to employ Western Region pilotmen for the short journey across to the former GWR station, but whatever the reasons, tender-first running became particularly common in the years following World War II.

Although it was hardly a unique occurrence, the sight of a '4F' running backwards at the head of a one coach train was, to say the least, unusual. ('4Fs' occasionally worked tender-first on the Somerset & Dorset line.) Engines ran with their chimneys facing towards Banbury, and this ensured that drivers could face "the right way" on the long climb up to Helmdon summit (the inconvenience of tender-first running did not matter so much when coasting downhill!).

The First Closures

In retrospect, the late 1940s and early 1950s were a time of complete stagnation in which no attempt was made to run the line economically, yet few people could imagine a time when rural branch lines such as the Banbury to Blisworth route would no longer exist. Railways were still seen as vital components of the national infrastructure, and the news that BR was considering withdrawal of the passenger service between Blisworth and Banbury came as a complete surprise. It was clear, however, that the limited train services between Blisworth and Banbury were attracting very few passengers, and there was, sadly, no case for retention of a rural branch line that had clearly outlived its useful life.

It was announced that the line from Banbury to Towcester would be closed from Monday 2nd July, 1951, and as this was a Monday, the last trains would run on the previous Saturday. The withdrawal of passenger services between Banbury and Towcester would entail the closure of Wappenham and Helmdon stations, but goods traffic would continue to be handled at those stations. The eastern section of the former Banbury & Northampton Junction Railway was not involved in the closure because it would continue to carry trains between Blisworth and Stratford-upon-Avon — at least for the time being.

Branch line closures were hardly a new phenomenon, and indeed, the "Big Four" railway companies had carried out extensive closure pro-

The last train from Banbury to Blisworth awaits the 'right away' at Banbury Merton Street on Saturday 30th June, 1951. Class '4F' 0–6–0, No. 44204 sports the Union Flag on its tender, while coach No. M20264 is adorned with the Royal Standard!

Lens of Sutton

Wappenham station looking west on the last day of passenger services — Saturday 30th June, 1951. Note the LMS 'Hawkseye' type nameplate (*left*) that had replaced the original nameboard prior to World War II.

Lens of Sutton

grammes as far back as the 1930s (90 lines were axed in 1930/31 alone).
However, there had been a pause in the pace of retraction and when, in the
years following World War II, British Railways initiated another substantial
pruning operation, there was an air of novelty about each fresh closure.
There was a feeling that the newly-nationalised railways had become pawns
of the government, and for these reasons the last day of the Banbury–
Cockley Brake–Towcester line was treated as a special occasion. Inevitably,
the line carried more travellers than usual during its final hours of operation, and the last train to serve Helmdon and Wappenham pulled out of
Banbury Merton Street behind flag-bedecked '4F' 0–6–0 No. 44204 on
Saturday 30th June, 1951; the locomotive ran tender-first, and its train
consisted of a solitary brake third.

Closure of the Towcester to Blisworth Line

Wappenham and Helmdon stations lost their goods services in the following October, but passenger traffic lingered on between Blisworth and
Stratford for a few more months. The end came on Saturday 5th April, 1952,
when the residual passenger service from Blisworth to Stratford-upon-Avon
was withdrawn, coincident with the closure of Towcester station. As in
1951, the last day was something of an occasion, and ironically, the final
service from Stratford to Blisworth conveyed extra coaches to accommodate
the additional travellers.

Headed by class '4F' 0–6–0 No. 44525, the five-coach train left Stratford-
upon-Avon with the town's Mayor at the controls, and small groups of
mourners witnessed its passage through country stations such as Blakesley
and Moreton Pinkney. At Towcester, a large crowd had gathered, and all too
soon the last train reached Blisworth; as it drew to a stand in the station's
platform, those watching the melancholy scene were conscious of the fact
that eighty-six years of railway history were coming to an end before their
very eyes. It was, in truth, the end of an era.

The abandoned line between Greens Norton Junction and Cockley Brake
was lifted in 1955, but with freight trains still running between Blisworth
and Broom Junction, the line through Towcester retained much of the
atmosphere of a "used" railway. Goods trains continued to operate over the
former Stratford-upon-Avon, Towcester & Midland Junction line between
Towcester and Ravenstone Wood Junction, and although the intermediate
goods station at Stoke Bruern was closed in July 1955, the line remained in
being as a through route for several more months.

The Ravenstone Wood line was closed "temporarily" in the Winter of
1957, and "officially" on 22nd June, 1958. Curiously, the new M1 motorway
bisected the doomed railway between Stoke Bruern and Ravenstone Wood,
but rather than sever the closed line, the motorway was carried overhead on
an expensive bridge! As far as can be ascertained, the last through goods
train passed over the line in May 1958, but the route was used thereafter as a
convenient parking place for spare coal wagons, and the connections at
Ravenstone Wood and Towcester remained in situ. The stored wagons
were removed around 1962, and the line was lifted shortly afterwards, this

Stanier 2−6−4T No. 42667 stands in the N&BJR platform at Banbury Merton Street on a Bletchley working. The hemispherical gas lamps replaced the original 'square' lanterns after World War II.   *Lens of Sutton*

The single platform station at Wappenham looking east towards Towcester in the 1950s. The overgrown track and damaged fences suggest that the photograph was taken several months after closure.   *Douglas Thompson*

operation being completed by 1964. Several bridges were removed in connection with the demolition work, but the recently-constructed M1 bridge was adapted for use as a cattle shelter by local farmers.

The Final Years

The subsequent history of the Northampton & Banbury Junction line is a sorry tale of piecemeal closure and abandonment. As usual in the case of freight-only lines, it is by no means easy to determine when the last movement of rolling stock actually took place, and this unsatisfactory situation is further obscured by the way in which the history of the N&BJR merged with that of the former East & West Junction line after 1910. It is necessary, therefore, to treat the erstwhile N&BJR and E&WJR lines as a single entity, and for further clarity, it would be sensible to show these final closure dates in tabular form (see *Table 6*).

Table 6

WITHDRAWAL OF FREIGHT SERVICES BETWEEN BROOM JN AND BLISWORTH, ETC.

section of line	date of closure
Towcester to Cockley Brake Jn	29th October, 1951
Towcester to Ravenstone Wood Jn	22nd June, 1958
Broom Jn to Stratford (Old Town)	13th June, 1960
Woodford West Jn to Blisworth Ironstone Siding	3rd February, 1964
Stratford-upon-Avon to Burton Dassett	1st March, 1965
Woodford to Byfield Ironstone Siding	1st March, 1965
Byfield Ironstone Siding to Fenny Compton	5th July, 1965

Confusingly, the "official" closures listed in *Table 6* were not necessarily the date of final closure, and in this context it is interesting to note that a railtour traversed the supposedly closed route to Stratford on 24th April, 1965, the section of line concerned remaining nominally "open" until 5th July, 1965. Such railtours had, in fact, brought a modicum of interest to the former S&MJ system in the years since closure to regular passenger traffic — on 5th October, 1963, for instance, a Midland & Great Northern Joint Railway Society tour had brought 'B12' 4–6–0 No. 61572 on to the Blisworth to Stratford line.

The spate of closures between 1960 and 1965 left just two sections of the S&MJ in regular use. These were a short section between Fenny Compton and Burton Dassett (reached via a new direct junction with the former GWR and used in connection with a nearby army camp), and a residual fragment of the N&BJ line from Blisworth to Blisworth ironstone quarries that had been retained to serve the premises of Richard Thomas & Baldwins Ltd.

Meanwhile, as the pace of rationalisation quickened throughout Britain, lines that had once provided connections for the Northampton & Banbury Junction Railway and its allies were themselves succumbing to closure — among them the Banbury to Verney Junction line which was closed in

December 1960, and the Northampton to Bedford route which followed its neighbours into oblivion in March 1962.

In 1966, the Blisworth line and its associated quarry lines were still in operation, and indeed, this little-known industrial network remained fairly busy, with no less than four steam locomotives in use. These included three 0–4–0 saddle tanks and one Hunslet 0–6–0, the full fleet being as follows:

Table 7

INDUSTRIAL LOCOMOTIVES AT RICHARD THOMAS & BALDWINS, BLISWORTH, c.1960

Name	*wheelbase*	*builders*	*date*
Siemens	0–4–0ST	Ebbw Vale Ironworks	1909
Ettrick	0–4–0ST	Hawthorn Leslie	1928
Blisworth	0–4–0ST	Andrew Barclay	1955
—	0–6–0ST	Hunslet	1940

The presence of this small industrial system on what was left of the N&BJR line ensured that the line remained of interest to enthusiasts long after the withdrawal of regular passenger services, but sadly, the closure of Richard Thomas & Baldwins' quarries at the end of September, 1967 brought about an abrupt termination of railway services on 30th September, 1967. On that sad day the history of the Northampton & Banbury Junction Railway finally drew to a close.

STRATFORD-ON-AVON, BANBURY AND BLISWORTH

THIRD CLASS ONLY

WEEKDAYS ONLY

Miles		a.m.	a.m.	SO a.m.	SX p.m.	p.m.	p.m.
—	**STRATFORD-ON-AVON** dep.	7 12	...	11 58	...	...	6 40
5¾	Ettington	7 24	...	12 11	...	...	6 53
9¾	Kineton	7 32	...	12 19	...	...	7 1
15¾	Fenny Compton	7 46	...	12 33	...	...	7 13
22¾	Byfield	7 59	...	12 46	4 45	...	7 26
26¼	Morton Pinkney	8 8	...	12 56	4 55	...	7 36
29¾	Blakesley	8 15	...	1 3	5 1	...	7 44
—	**BANBURY** dep.	...	10 40	...	...	4 45	...
3¾	Farthinghoe	...	10 49	...	...	4 54	...
8½	Helmdon	...	11 2	...	...	5 7	...
12¼	Wappenham	...	11 11	...	...	5 15	...
16¼	Towcester	8 25	11 21	1 11	5 10	5 23	7 52
—	**BLISWORTH** arr.	8 36	11 30	1 22	5 20	5 32	8 2
½	50 **NORTHAMPTON** arr.	8 55	11 55	2 3	...	6 8	8 20
½	50 **LONDON (Euston)** arr.	10 21	3c41	4 15	...	7 45	10 57

WEEKDAYS ONLY

Miles		a.m.	a.m.	SO a.m.	SX a.m.	p.m.	p.m.
—	50 **LONDON (Euston)** dep.	6 40	...	11 32	11 32	4 35	...
—	50 **NORTHAMPTON**	8 25	9 0	1 30	2 32	5 30	6 14
—	**BLISWORTH** dep.	8 55	9 31	2 0	4 0	6 0	6 50
4	Towcester	9A10	9 41	2 10	4B15	6 10	7 0
8	Wappenham	...	9 51	...	...	6 22	...
11¾	Helmdon	...	10 0	...	...	6 32	...
16½	Farthinghoe	...	10 12	...	...	6 47	...
20¼	**BANBURY** arr.	...	10 20	...	...	6 56	...
8¼	Blakesley	9 17	...	2 19	4 23	...	7 7
11¾	Morton Pinkney	9 27	...	2 26	4 30	...	7 14
15¼	Byfield	9 38	...	2 36	4 39	...	7 26
22	Fenny Compton	9 51	...	2 48	...	...	7 39
28¼	Kineton	10 6	...	3 2	...	..	7 51
32¼	Ettington	10 15	...	3 11	...	...	7 59
38	**STRATFORD-ON-AVON** arr.	10 26	...	3 22	...	...	8 8

A—Arrives 9.4 a.m. B—Arrives 4.10 p.m. C—Arrives 2.40 p.m. on Saturdays commencing June 24th. SX—Saturdays excepted. SO—Saturdays only.

The British Rail June 1950 passenger timetable for the line.

The Railway Today

Although the Northampton & Banbury Junction Railway has been closed and lifted, its course can be followed by road or on foot, and indeed, much of the former N&BJR route has now become an attractive (though unofficial footpath) through rural Northamptonshire.

Most buildings have been demolished, and at Towcester the station site is occupied by modern factory premises. The large girder bridge that formerly spanned Watling Street has been taken down, and motorists driving past on the busy A5 find it hard to believe that Towcester ever had a station!

Moving westwards, the recently-completed Towcester by-pass has severed the trackbed near Greens Norton Junction, but a substantial section of embankment remains in situ to the south of the new road. From Greens Norton Junction the railway continues, as a grass-covered track, towards Wappenham, and the deep cutting near Abthorpe remains intact.

Wappenham station has been removed, and its site is occupied by a modern bungalow, though the nearby twin-span overbridge still stands as a visual reminder of the vanished railway. Continuing westwards, much of the trackbed is still extant, and three overbridges near Wappenham village have survived. Beyond, the route survives as a lonely track, but the cutting near Astwell Castle has beeen filled with accumulated rubbish, and this unsightly dumping operation has effectively buried one of the line's distinctive twin-arched bridges.

At Helmdon, the station yard is used by a coach operator, and the goods shed and weigh house remain intact. Sadly, the station building has been removed, its site being occupied by another bungalow. From Helmdon the abandoned trackbed passes beneath the still-extant Great Central viaduct (itself trackless and derelict), while at Cockley Brake the former junction is partially obscured by dense vegetation that, in places, acts as an effective deterrent to all but the most active walkers.

Little remains at Banbury Merton Street, which lost its passenger services in December 1960 when the line to Verney Junction was closed. Goods traffic lingered on for a few more months, but in December 1963 the former LNWR branch was closed between Banbury and Buckingham and thereafter Merton Street could be reached only from the adjacent Great Western station. The former Buckinghamshire Railway terminus was finally closed in June 1966, and the erstwhile GWR–LNWR transfer siding was subsequently lifted.

A Note on Signalling

Although there has already been some mention of signalling and signal boxes, there is scope for a more detailed analysis of these aspects of the N&BJR story, and the following notes may be useful to modellers (and others) seeking further details of the minutae of railway operation.

In Northampton & Banbury Junction days the single line between Blisworth and Towcester was worked on the staff-and-ticket system, whereby drivers were allowed to follow one or more trains onto the single line on receipt of written authorisation. This system (in effect a variant of the

This 3-doll bracket signal carrying a home and two subsidiary arms was situated at the west end of Towcester station. The main post is possibly of Gloucester Wagon Company origin, but the angle brackets and signal arms are of Midland Railway design; note the differing finials which underline the hybrid nature of N&BJR signalling in the LMS era. *Lens of Sutton*

Towcester signal cabin was a standard Gloucester Wagon Company design, with that company's characteristic finials, barge boards and fenestration. The box was, however, adapted for use on this restricted site being between two running lines. *Lens of Sutton*

"divisible staff" system) was useful when excursions or other workings were all heading in the same direction. The electric train staff was later installed on the Towcester to Blisworth section, and this equipment was also used on the remainder of the line to Cockley Brake.

The staff sections were Blisworth–Towcester, Towcester–Greens Norton, Greens Norton–Helmdon, Helmdon–Cockley Brake, and Cockley Brake–Banbury but it was possible for the Blisworth to Towcester section to be divided into two, and this expedient (made possible by a temporary block post at Tiffield) was used during the busy Grafton Hunt period. As we have seen, the line was later worked on a much simpler system, with block sections from Blisworth to Towcester, Towcester to Cockley Brake and Cockley Brake to Banbury.

Small companies such as the Northampton & Banbury Junction or East & West Junction railways usually purchased their signalling equipment from specialist manufacturers such as McKenzie & Holland or the Gloucester Wagon Company, and there is both written and photographic evidence to suggest that the N&BJR purchased signals and signal boxes from the Gloucester Company. The gabled signal cabins at Blisworth and Towcester were standard GWCo products with that company's characteristic finials, barge boards and fenestration, and these boxes survived into the BR era as tangible reminders of the Northampton & Banbury Junction and Stratford-upon-Avon & Midland Junction eras.

N&BJR signalling underwent many upheavals after 1910, and more especially after 1923 — when the LMS introduced many Midland-style signalling components. By the 1930s, N&BJR signalling had become an amalgam of Midland, LNWR, S&MJR and N&BJR practice, and it could be said, with very little exaggeration, that no two N&BJR signals were the same! Moreover, Blisworth and Towcester were provided with some relatively complex signalling systems (at least by branch line standards) and two, three, or even four doll configurations could be found in or around these two stations.

At Blisworth, the two terminal roads were signalled for bi-directional working, with home and starter signals for each platform. The westernmost platform face (which seems to have been the main departure platform) was provided with a single post starter, but the other side of the station was equipped with a bracket signal, giving trains the choice of two routes once they had been given the right away; both signals were of LNWR pattern, with square-capped posts and corrugated arms. As usual on North Western signals, the vertical white stripe across the red face of the arm was situated towards the middle (as opposed to the end) of the arms.

There were advanced starters at the end of the run-round loop (which, as mentioned in Chapter Five was *beyond* the platform limits) and these too were of LNWR pattern. In the up direction, incoming trains were regulated by two 3-doll bracket signals (one of which was at the station throat while the other was near the passenger platform) and in this way drivers knew whether they were about to enter the left or the right-hand terminal platform or (alternatively) the long exchange siding that linked the N&BJR and LNWR stations.

By present-day standards Blisworth would have been considered over-signalled and it is surprising that, in view of the rationalisation carried out elsewhere on the N&BJR line, the LMS did not effect a major simplification. In the event, the terminus retained its complex semaphore signalling for many years, but by the time of closure the LNWR lower quadrants had been replaced by a limited number of modern upper quadrant semaphores. This simplified system was entirely appropriate for a line that carried only a few trains each way.

The signalling at Towcester was even more complicated than that at Blisworth, though this complexity is understandable when one reflects that the station had junctions at each end, with a correspondingly large number of route permutations.

In common with other parts of the London Midland & Scottish Railway the N&BJR section was progressively re-signalled with upper quadrant semaphores, but there was nevertheless a lengthy transition period, and some archaic wooden-posted lower quadrant signals survived for many years alongside their more modern counterparts.

Midland-type signalling at Towcester. The up junction signal (left) incorporates standard MR brackets and spiked finials, but the two arms are possibly of Gloucester Wagon Company origin; their spectacle plates are not of MR appearance, though the left hand arm may be a Derby product. The down home signal (right) is also a hybrid, its post being of MR design while its finials and arms are of some other manufacture.
Lens of Sutton

Helmdon station site was used as a coach depot after its final closure, seen here with a Bedford OB 26-seater in the yard.   *Lens of Sutton*

Another view of Helmdon after closure, showing the distinctive station building and ornate chimneys to advantage.   *Lens of Sutton*

Appendix One
Table of Distances

LOCATION	m	ch	m	ch	m	ch
Blisworth	00	00				
Towcester	04	15	00	00		
Wappenham	08	07	03	72		
Helmdon	11	59	07	44		
Cockley Brake	15	01	10	66	00	00
Farthinghoe	16	50	12	35	01	49
Banbury	20	43	16	28	05	42

Appendix Two
N&BJR Station Masters

The Northampton & Banbury Junction Railway had just four stations, and opportunities for promotion were severely limited. Not surprisingly, there was considerable continuity in terms of station masters, and this continuity is underlined by the following table. For completeness, Farthinghoe has also been included, although that station was of course on the LNWR section of the Blisworth–Banbury route.

	1874	1890	1906	1912	1924
Blisworth	E. Stanton	Wllm. White	Harry Ashby	Albert Gilkes	Fred Parker
Towcester	F.B. Venner	John Owen	Thos. Holton	Thos. Holton	Wllm. Leigh
Wappenham	J. Pinfold	G. Brown	G. Brown	Harry Ashby	Thos. Holton
Helmdon	C. Stephens	G. Brown	G. Brown	Harry Ashby	Fred Smart
Farthinghoe	n/a	G. Tustain	Wllm. Tustain	Wllm. Tustain	John Harris

Bibliography of Secondary Source Material

The Northampton & Banbury Junction Railway, East & West Junction Railway or other constituents of the S&MJR have not enjoyed much attention from railway historians, and it is useful, therefore, to append a short bibliography for the benefit of those seeking further information on these hitherto neglected rural lines. For completeness, some S&MJ material has been included on the following list, for as we have seen, it has proved difficult to treat the N&BJR as an entirely separate entity. The presence of a title on this list does not necessarily imply that the work in question has been used as a source, although a considerable amount of incidental data was obtained from some of the following works.

J.M. Dunn	*The Stratford-upon-Avon & Midland Junction Railway* (1952) *passim.*
Arthur Jordan	*The Stratford-upon-Avon & Midland Junction Railway* (1982).
Herbert Evans	*Highways & Byways in Northamptonshire & Rutland* (1918).
John Steane	*The Northamptonshire Landscape* (1974).
C.R.H. Simpson	The Northampton & Banbury Junction Railway, *The Locomotive Magazine*, November 1946, pp. 171–75.
D.S. Barrie	The Stratford-upon-Avon & Midland Junction Railway, *The LMS Railway Magazine*, April 1933, pp. 235–42.
Francis Whellan	*The History, Topography & Directory of Northamptonshire 1874.*
G. Sekon	Illustrated Interview with Mr Russell Willmott, *The Railway Magazine*, April 1910, pp. 265–76.
Bill Ibbott	Blakesley Station, SMJR, *Railway Modeller*, March 1968, pp. 84–5.
Vivien Thompson	Building Blakesley, *Railway Modeller*, July 1968, pp. 200–1.
J.J. Davis	Byfield and Stratford Signal Boxes, *Model Railway News*, March 1963, p. 121.
W. Potts	*A History of Banbury* (1958).

Index